C. H.

Spiritual Leadership

C. H. SPURGEON

# on Spiritual Leadership

Steve Miller

MOODY PUBLISHERS
CHICAGO

*To every leader and aspiring leader*

*who desires to grow toward greater*

*Christlikeness and longs to inspire*

*others to do the same*

# CONTENTS

∽

## Growing Toward
## Greater Spiritual Leadership

∞

The best spiritual leaders are those who are always learning. They're the ones who ask, How can I do this better? How can I have a greater impact? How can I inspire the people around me upward and onward in their Christian growth? How can I glorify God more?

If your desire is to grow into a better leader, these are the kinds of questions you want to ask. And one of the best ways to get answers, in addition to learning what the Bible says about leadership, is to see good spiritual leadership in action.

The Lord Jesus Christ Himself knew the great value of a role model. That's why He gave hands-on training to His disciples for three years, day in and day out. He didn't merely give them some textbooks to study; He lived out and taught spiritual leadership before their eyes.

The apostle Paul did the same with his son in the faith, Timothy. He demonstrated what a ministry leader looked like in real life and provided Timothy with descriptive portraits of godly spiritual leadership in the pastoral epistles of the New Testament. And to the Christians in the ancient city of Corinth, Paul wrote, "Imitate me, just as I also imitate Christ" (1 Corinthians 11:1). Simply put, we can learn a lot by watching a good role model who is following the ultimate role model, Jesus Christ.

In this book, we're going to see spiritual leadership in action in the life and words of Charles Haddon Spurgeon. Spurgeon's influence as a minister and leader is legendary—his ministry began in the early 1850s, and from 1861 to 1891 he preached to some 6,000 people every Sunday morning in the Metropolitan Tabernacle in London. Everywhere he traveled, crowds of 10,000 to 20,000 would gather to hear him. With the help of his church leaders, Spurgeon organized and ran several evangelistic, educational, and social ministries, including the Pastors' College, the Stockwell Orphanage (first for boys, and then an additional wing for girls), the Old Ladies Home (for elderly women who had no family to provide support), the Colportage Ministry (for the distribution of Christian literature and tracts), the Pastors' Aid Society, and the Poor Ministers' Clothing Society. Before his death, his many books had sold into the multiple millions of copies, and his writings had been translated into thirty-plus languages. His sermons alone fill about seventy hefty volumes.

But more importantly, Spurgeon was passionately committed to serving God and caring for God's people. His was a life characterized by unceasing prayer, steadfast faith, powerful preaching, and extraordinary compassion for the hurting and the unsaved. Those who served alongside him appreciated his generous heart and genuine humility. It is these qualities that made Spurgeon a great spiritual leader—not the numbers of people he attracted, the extent of his ministries, or the books he published.

Within the pages of this book, we'll look at several key qualities that stood out in Spurgeon's life—qualities that every spiritual leader should have. Each chapter will conclude with a closing thought from Spurgeon on the topic, whether given "On His Knees," "With His Pen," or "In the Pulpit." By no means is this an exhaustive study; a complete collection of Spurgeon's sermons and writings on leadership and related issues would easily fill several volumes. Rather, this is a carefully selected assortment of quotations designed to encourage you and give you ideas you can put into practice as you fulfill your leadership responsibilities. Spurgeon's words are shown as printed in the original sources and by compilers and biographers, maintaining the emphases of the original sermons, prayers, and writings. A small number of adaptations have been made for editorial consistency.

Also, while a good portion of Spurgeon's instructions on leadership were originally directed toward pastors, the principles given in this book are useful for virtually any area of leadership—whether you are a teacher, missionary, group leader, ministry helper, program director, or Bible college or seminary student who aspires to become a spiritual leader.

My prayer is that as you read through this book, you'll find yourself inspired toward greater leadership, greater usefulness by God, and a greater impact on all those around you. If that is your desire, I know you'll find C. H. Spurgeon a welcome mentor in your daily service to our Lord.

CHAPTER   ONE

# <sup>A</sup> Passion
## *for* Prayer

"PRAY WITHOUT CEASING."

—1 THESSALONIANS 5:17

As a busy minister, Charles Haddon Spurgeon cherished the rare opportunities that allowed him time to visit with close friends. On one such occasion, when Dr. Theodore Cuyler of Brooklyn came to England, Spurgeon invited him for a walk through the woods—another pastime Spurgeon loved yet seldom had time for. During the walk, Spurgeon surprised his guest with a rather unexpected comment. Their conversation must have been lighthearted and even mirthful, for suddenly Spurgeon stopped and said, "Come, Theodore, let us thank God for laughter." Later, when Dr. Cuyler spoke of this particular visit, he said, "That was how he lived. From a jest to a prayer meant with him the breadth of a straw."[1]

That incident is but one of many that demonstrate Spurgeon's spontaneity when it came to prayer. What stood out above all in Spurgeon's life as a minister—even more than his extraordinary giftedness for preaching—was his diligence in prayer. Not only was he faithful in the practice of prayer, he also bathed all of life in prayer. In the introduction to *C. H. Spurgeon's Prayers*, Dinsdale T. Young observes that "prayer was the instinct of his soul, and the atmosphere of his life."[2]

Spurgeon himself once told a friend, "I always feel it well just to put a few words of prayer between everything I do."[3] He lived out the biblical admonishment to pray unceasingly, which had a profound impact on his ministry.

A few months after Spurgeon's death, the famous American preacher and evangelist D. L. Moody spoke to Spurgeon's congregation at the Metropolitan Tabernacle and shared with them about his first visit to the building twenty-five years earlier. He had come to London to hear Spurgeon preach, and what impressed him most was not the beautiful congregational singing or the powerful sermon, but Spurgeon's heart-stirring prayer. Dr. John Cairns, another noted minister, said he exulted in hearing Spurgeon's sermons, yet he exulted even more in hearing his prayers.

## −UNCEASING COMMUNION WITH GOD−

What made Spurgeon's prayers so luminous, so memorable? Those who observed his life up close commented on his perpetual private communion with God, and it was the intimate spiritual richness of these times alone with the Lord that overflowed into Spurgeon's public prayers and led people to feel as if he were taking them into the very portals of heaven through his petitions. Spurgeon's ongoing inclination toward prayer is evident in these words:

∽

*I cannot help praying. If I were not allowed to utter a word all day long, that would not affect my praying. If I could not have five minutes that I might spend in prayer by myself, I should pray all the same. Minute by minute, moment by moment, somehow or other, my heart must commune with God. Prayer has become as essential to me as the heaving of my lungs and the beating of my pulse.*[4]

∽

We've all heard Scripture's command to "pray without ceasing" (1 Thessalonians 5:17). But what exactly does that mean? Spurgeon explained it this way:

∞

*Our Lord meant by saying men ought always to pray, that they ought to be always in the spirit of prayer, always ready to pray. Like the old knights, always in warfare, not always on their steeds dashing forward with their lances in rest to unhorse an adversary, but always wearing their weapons where they could readily reach them, and always ready to encounter wounds or death for the sake of the cause which they championed. Those grim warriors often slept in their armour; so even when we sleep, we are still to be in the spirit of prayer, so that if perchance we wake in the night, we may still be with God. Our soul, having received the divine centripetal influence which makes it seek its heavenly centre, should be evermore naturally rising towards God Himself. Our heart is to be like those beacons and watchtowers which were prepared along the coast of England when the invasion of the Armada was hourly expected, not always blazing, but with the wood always dry, and the match always there, the whole pile being ready to blaze up at the appointed moment.[5]*

∞

What would our lives be like if we were to find prayer as natural as breathing, as Spurgeon did? Or if we were to have the "match" of prayer always ready? What effect would this have on our ministry endeavors? Were we to draw near to the Lord with such persistence, we would come to know Him and His ways such that we would become more and more of one heart and one mind with Him and thus reflect Him more clearly to those whom we lead.

## –GIVING CREDIT WHERE IT'S DUE–

Many reasons have been given for the tremendous influence of Spurgeon's ministry, with the credit usually being attributed to the abilities or cleverness of the man himself. But Spurgeon made it clear that any success he knew was the direct result of a complete dependence upon God through prayer, especially the intercessory prayers of his church:

∽

*The fact is, the secret of all ministerial success lies in prevalence at the mercy-seat.*[6]

*I stand here to confess frankly that from my inmost heart I attribute the large prosperity which God has given to this church vastly more to the prayers of the people than to anything that God may have given to me.*[7]

∽

Spurgeon saw prayer very much as a lifeline to God, a lifeline for which there was no substitute, and which, if neglected, would impair the effectiveness of a minister and church. Indeed, in everything, we are utterly dependent upon God and His free-flowing grace, and what better way is there to be at the receiving end of His provision than by kneeling at His feet in free-flowing prayer?

## —The Greatest Weapon—

To Spurgeon (and this should be true for any spiritual leader), there was nothing ordinary about prayer. He had a lofty view of prayer, and rightly so. In his sermons, he endeavored to instill in his congregation both a reverential awe and an unshakeable confidence in the power of prayer. These are among his exhortations:

∞

*My own soul's conviction is that prayer is the grandest power in the entire universe, that it has a more omnipotent force than electricity, attraction, gravitation, or any other of those secret forces which men have called by name, but which they do not understand.*[8]

*If any of you should ask me for an epitome of the Christian religion, I should say it is in that one word—prayer.*[9]

*Prayer is the master-weapon. We should be greatly wise if we used it more, and did so with a more specific purpose.*[10]

∞

## –PRAYER'S PLACE IN THE LEADER'S LIFE–

Spurgeon's recognition of the priority of prayer came early in his ministry. Biographer W. Y. Fullerton observed that even at the age of sixteen, when Spurgeon began to preach in small rural English churches, he would arise early in the morning to pray and read the Bible.[11] Spurgeon had this to say about the absolute necessity of prayer in a minister's life:

∞

*Never account prayer second to preaching. No doubt prayer in the Christian church is as precious as the utterance of the gospel. To speak to God for men is a part of the Christian priesthood that should never be despised.*[12]

*The minister who does not earnestly pray over his work must surely be a vain and conceited man. He acts as if he thought himself sufficient of himself, and therefore needed not to appeal to God.*[13]

∞

Spurgeon often chastised ministers who were more concerned about their outward appearances to men and thus put greater emphasis on the external aspects of their ministry, such as preaching. Many of the ministers in Spurgeon's era expended great effort in producing eloquent sermons that offered scant spiritual nourishment to the hearers, and they spent little time in their private prayer closets. As a result, their ministries lacked life and power, and tragically, the attendance in their churches declined.

## –Prayer: An Intimate Encounter–

What is it about prayer that makes it so special, so essential? Spurgeon recognized prayer as more than mere thoughts or words lifted heavenward, but as an intimate encounter with the all-caring Father and all-powerful God of the universe:

∞

*Prayer links us with the Eternal, the Omnipotent, the Infinite, and hence it is our chief resort. Resolve to serve the Lord, and to be faithful to His cause, for then you may boldly appeal to Him for succor. Be sure that you are with God, and then you may be sure that God is with you.*[14]

*We do not bow the knee merely because it is a duty, and a commendable spiritual exercise, but because we believe that, into the ear of the eternal God, we speak our wants, and that His ear is linked with a heart feeling for us, and a hand working on our behalf. To us, true prayer is true power.*[15]

*Because God is the living God, He can hear; because He is a loving God, He will hear; because He is our covenant God, He has bound Himself to hear.*[16]

∞

God is always a ready listener, eager to hear our footsteps approach His throne. But are we equally eager to bring ourselves into His presence? If we as spiritual leaders fail to possess an enthusiasm for spending time with God in prayer, we cannot expect those who follow us to catch that enthusiasm.

## –ENTERING GOD'S TREASURE-HOUSE–

Spurgeon painted a beautiful picture of the multifaceted benefits of prayer when he said,

∞

*The very act of prayer is a blessing. To pray is as it were to bathe oneself in a purling cool stream, and so to escape from the heat of earth's summer sun. To pray is to mount on eagle's wings above the clouds and get into the clear heaven where God dwells. To pray is to enter the treasure-house of God and to enrich oneself out of an inexhaustible storehouse.*

21

> *To pray is to grasp heaven in one's arms, to embrace the Deity within one's soul, and to feel one's body made a temple of the Holy Ghost. Apart from the answer, prayer is in itself a benediction. To pray is to cast off your burdens, it is to tear away your rags, it is to shake off your diseases, it is to be filled with spiritual vigour, it is to reach the highest point of Christian health. God give us to be much in the holy art of arguing with God in prayer.*[17]

∞

The kind of prayer life we have will be outwardly evident to those around us, for prayer brings very real changes in us, as stated above. As Spurgeon said, "To pray . . . is to reach the highest point of Christian health." Are we at the highest point of our vitality? Only then can we expect the highest results when we carry out the responsibilities we bear as spiritual leaders.

## −A WELL-WORN PRAYER CLOSET−

As noted earlier, Spurgeon's public prayers stirred the hearts of his listeners as much or even more so than his preaching. But these prayers were only the tip of the iceberg, buoyed upward by the unseen depth and breadth of his private times alone with God. Consider his words about private prayer—words that anyone in a position of spiritual leadership would do well to take to heart:

∞

*It may scarcely be needful to commend to you the sweet uses of private devotion, and yet I cannot forbear. To you, as the ambassadors of God, the mercy-seat has a virtue beyond all estimate; the more familiar you are with the court of heaven the better shall you discharge your heavenly trust. Among all the formative influences which go to make up a man honored of God in the ministry, I know of none more mighty than his own familiarity with the mercy-seat. All that a college course can do for a student is coarse and external compared with the spiritual and delicate refinement obtained by communion with God. While the unformed minister is revolving upon the wheel of preparation, prayer is the tool of the great potter by which He molds the vessel. All our libraries and studies are mere emptiness compared with our closets. We grow, we wax mighty, we prevail in private-prayer.[18]*

*You cannot pray too long in private. The more you are on your knees alone the better.[19]*

*How much of blessing we may have missed through remissness in supplication we can scarcely guess, and none of us can know how poor we are in comparison with what we might have been if we had lived habitually nearer to God in prayer. We not only ought to pray more, but we must.*[20]

*Neglect of private prayer is the locust which devours the strength of the church.*[21]

∞

One Sunday Spurgeon revealed to his congregation, "I have not preached this morning half as much as I have prayed. For every word that I have spoken, I have prayed two words silently to God."[22]

Because private prayer is a hidden part of our life, it's all too easy to neglect it. After all, who will know whether we have taken the time to be alone with God? But we can be certain that any weakness in our personal prayer life will eventually manifest itself in a corresponding weakness in our public ministry life. By contrast, a strong prayer life will result in a stronger ministry.

## −PRAYING WITH THE RIGHT HEART−

It's also vital to recognize that the mere act of praying is not enough to unlock the door to heaven's storehouses of blessings. When we pray, we need to consider the attitude of our hearts. Thus Spurgeon urged his fellow ministers:

∞

*When you are engaged in prayer, plead your strength, and you will get nothing; then plead your weakness, and you will prevail. There is no better plea with Divine love than weakness and pain; nothing can so prevail with the great heart of God as for your heart to faint and swoon. The man who rises in prayer to tears and agony, and feels all the while as if he could not pray, and yet must pray— he is the man who will see the desire of his soul. Do not mothers always care most for the tiniest child, or for that one which is most sick? Do we not spend the greatest care upon that one of our children which has the least use of its limbs; and is it not true that our weakness holds God's strength, and leads Him to bow His omnipotence to our rescue?*[23]

*Our addresses to the throne of grace must be solemn and humble, not flippant and loud, or formal and careless. The colloquial form of speech is out of place before the Lord; we must bow reverently and with deepest awe. We may speak boldly with God, but still He is in heaven and we are upon earth, and we are to avoid presumption. In supplication we are peculiarly before the throne of the Infinite, and as the courtier in the king's palace puts on another mien*

25

*and another manner than that which he exhibits to
his fellow courtiers, so should it be with us.*[24]

*Only that prayer which comes from our heart can
get to God's heart.*[25]

∞

## −Challenges Faced in Prayer−

When it comes to the art of prayer, many of us feel inadequate.
We often find ourselves struggling in prayer, wishing we could
master it better. We may find solace in knowing that even
Spurgeon, with his vast experience in the practice of prayer,
included himself among those who feel inadequate in this
spiritual discipline. At one point he said, "I usually feel more
dissatisfied with my prayers than anything else I do."[26]

Another common frustration we may face is the challenge of
making time for prayer in the midst of a busy schedule. The
demands of everyday life clamor for our attention, and all too
often prayer falls two, three, or even several notches down our
list of priorities. Spurgeon commented:

∞

*Sometimes we think we are too busy to pray. That
is a great mistake, for praying is a saving of time.
You remember Luther's remark, "I have so much to
do today that I shall never get through it with less*

*than three hours' prayer." . . . If we have no time we must make time, for if God has given us time for secondary duties, He must have given us time for primary ones, and to draw near to Him is a primary duty, and we must let nothing set it on one side. Your other engagements will run smoothly if you do not forget your engagement with God.*[27]

∞

That's not to say our private prayers need to be as lengthy as Martin Luther's. The point is that serious demands upon our life call for serious prayers. No matter how many priorities crowd our to-do list, prayer is always the ultimate priority. After our time alone with God—however short or long it is—we can continue through the day as Spurgeon did, communing with God moment by moment, hour by hour throughout the day, living in a ready spirit of prayer. And taking the time to pray first is indeed a "saving of time," for there's something about prayer that helps us to get God's perspective on our day, prioritize our obligations, and get a clearer sense of what we need to do and how it should be done.

But what about those times when we just don't feel like praying? When we feel as if the spiritual well has run dry, when discouragement tells us it's just not worth the effort, when anger has set a strong foothold upon our hearts? What if our emotions or circumstances lead us to say, "I just don't feel like talking to God right now"? Spurgeon offers this solution:

∞

*I believe that when we cannot pray, it is time that we prayed more than ever. And if you answer, "But how can that be?" I would say, pray to pray. Pray for prayer. Pray for the spirit of supplication. Do not be content to say, "I would pray if I could." No, but if you cannot pray, pray till you can.*[28]

*If your heart be cold in prayer, do not restrain prayer until your heart warms, but pray your soul unto heat by the help of the ever-blessed Spirit, who helpeth our infirmities. If the iron be hot then hammer it, and if it be cold, hammer it till you heat it. Never cease in prayer for any reason.*[29]

∞

In the book of Psalms, we see a recurring pattern: Many of the prayers or psalms begin as laments of discouragement, then gradually turn into songs of praise. There's something about bringing our cares to God that comforts and reassures us. As Spurgeon said, "One night alone in prayer might make us new men, changed from poverty of soul to spiritual wealth, from trembling to triumphing."[30]

There may be times, of course, when we find it difficult to articulate our thoughts to God. At such times, the Holy Spirit can intercede for us, or even simple tears can.

∞

*A groan cometh not from the lips, but from the heart. A groan then is a part of prayer which we owe to the Holy Ghost, and the same is true of all the prayer which wells up from the deep fountains of our inner life. . . . This deep groundswell of desire, this tidal motion of the lifefloods is caused by the Holy Spirit. His work is never superficial, but always deep and inward.*[31]

*You can draw near to God even though you cannot say a word. A prayer may be crystallised in a tear. A tear is enough water to float a desire to God.*[32]

∞

## –AWAITING THE ANSWERS–

Perhaps the most mysterious aspect of prayer is God's response. How will He answer our prayers? Sometimes the response isn't what we expect. Or when the answer doesn't come, we wonder why. Or perhaps we're oblivious to the answer because we're unaware of how God wants to work in our life. As we wait upon God, we cannot help but wonder about *when* and *how* He will respond, or *why* He responded in a certain way. That's when we need to remember that God's wisdom and love are perfect, and, when we pray, we are to let go of our concerns and yield them into His hands, which are infinitely more capable than our own. Spurgeon shared this about God's timing in relation to answering our prayers:

∞

*Frequently the richest answers are not the speediest. . . . A prayer may be all the longer on its voyage because it is bringing us a heavier freight of blessing. Delayed answers are not only trials of faith, but they give us an opportunity of honouring God by our steadfast confidence in Him under apparent repulses.*[33]

*God's answers have never come too soon nor yet too late.*[34]

∞

When we find ourselves feeling uncertain about the future, rather than look ahead in fear, we can look back to the past and recall God's unceasing faithfulness in caring for us:

∞

*The Christian may do well sometimes to look backward . . . the retrospect will help him to be humble, it will urge him to be faithful. He may look back with satisfaction to the glorious hour when first he saw the Lord, when spiritual life for the first time quickened his dead soul. Then he may look back through all the changes of his life, to his troubles and his joys. I bid you stand upon the hill-top of your present experience and look back upon the past . . . that you may . . . [declare] in the language of the Psalmist, "I love the Lord, because he hath heard my voice and my supplication."* [35]

*Your prayers were innumerable; you asked for countless mercies, and they have all been given. Only look at yourself; are not you adorned and bejeweled with mercies as thick as the stars?* [36]

∽

And in one of his own prayers following a sermon, Spurgeon acknowledged,

∽

*O Lord, in looking back we are obliged to remember with the greatest gratitude the many occasions in which Thou hast heard our cry. We have been brought into deep distress, and our heart has sunk within us, and then have we cried to Thee and Thou hast never refused to hear us. The prayers of our lusts Thou hast rejected, but the prayers of our necessities Thou hast granted. Not one good thing hath failed of all that Thou hast promised.* [37]

∽

31

Indeed, God never fails. Though we don't understand our trials or circumstances, we can take confidence in knowing He can see them—and even beyond them—with perfect clarity. It is this confidence that gives us the strength to persevere, and the trait of perseverance will prove a valuable asset for those times when the difficulties inherent in our responsibilities as ministry leaders weigh heavily upon us.

## –The Powerhouse of a Church–

Spurgeon's convictions about the necessity of private prayer were exceedingly strong, and his convictions about the necessity of a prayerful church were equally strong. When he toured friends and guests through the Metropolitan Tabernacle, he would take them to the prayer room in the basement, where people could be found on their knees, offering up intercessory petitions to God. Spurgeon would tell his visitors, "Here is the powerhouse of this church." And in his sermons, Spurgeon pleaded often for his congregation to uphold him and the church in prayer. We, too, would gain much by urging our fellow church members to pray as a community. Consider Spurgeon's urgent words:

*A prayerful church is a powerful church. I think there will be less fault to find with the ministry when there shall be less fault to find with believers in their closets.*[38]

*If we were stronger in faith, mightier in prayer, more fervent in heart, more holy in life, who can tell how much we might effect for our age.*[39]

*The condition of the church may be very accurately gauged by its prayer meetings. So is the prayer meeting a grace-ometer, and from it we may judge of the amount of divine working among a people. If God be near a church, it must pray. And if He be not there, one of the first tokens of His absence will be slothfulness in prayer.*[40]

*Truly I wish that all pastors could always, without doubt, assume that they enjoyed the perpetual prayers of those under their charge.*[41]

*How often have I said, "All our strength lies in prayer!"*[42]

∽

## –A FINAL WORD ON PRAYER–

The ministry of Charles Spurgeon and the congregation at the Metropolitan Tabernacle reached far beyond the walls of the massive structure to countries all over the globe. Never before had a church drawn such large crowds, never before had a minister been more widely published and in so many languages. Travelers who came to London from around the world considered a stop at Metropolitan Tabernacle to be equally obligatory as stops at Westminster Abbey and St. Paul's Cathedral. The kingdom of God was extended mightily through this ministry, with countless multitudes coming to receive Christ as their Savior—and Spurgeon said all of it was the direct result of prayer . . . his own private prayers, and the ongoing intercessory prayers of the congregation. He saw the spiritual health of a church—and an individual—as being inextricably linked to prayer: "I know of no better thermometer to your spiritual temperature than this, the measure of the intensity of your prayer."[43]

# SPURGEON on His Knees

LORD JESUS, take from us now everything that would hinder the closest communion with God. Any wish or desire that might hamper us in prayer remove, we pray Thee. Any memory of either sorrow or care that might hinder the fixing of our affection wholly on our God, take it away now. What have we to do with idols any more? Thou hast seen and observed us. Thou knowest where the difficulty lies. Help us against it, and may we now come boldly, not into the Holy Place alone, but into the Holiest of all, where we should not dare to come if our great Lord had not rent the veil, sprinkled the mercy-seat with His own blood, and bidden us enter. . . .

Come, Holy Spirit, we do know Thee; Thou hast often overshadowed us. Come, more fully take possession of us. Standing now as we feel we are right up at the mercy-seat our very highest prayer is for perfect holiness, complete consecration, entire cleansing from every evil. Take our heart, our head, our hands, our feet, and use us all for Thee.[44]

# CHAPTER TWO

# A Faith
*that*
# Endures

"THE LORD IS MY ROCK AND MY FORTRESS AND MY DELIVERER; MY GOD, MY STRENGTH, IN WHOM I WILL TRUST."

—PSALM 18:2

*Childlike.* That's not a word most people associate with greatness or superior leadership. Words like *courageous, strong, wise, steadfast,* and *confident* might come to mind . . . but not *childlike.* Yet that's exactly what Dr. E. W. Hoyt considered to be among C. H. Spurgeon's more outstanding qualities as a leader. "Childlike credulity" is how he described it.

Hoyt knew Spurgeon well; the two were good friends who talked often about the many ministries under Spurgeon's care. Here's how one biographical source elaborated on Hoyt's choice of words:

Childlike credulity! Spurgeon expected the Almighty, as a loving heavenly Father, to meet all the necessities of His child. Telling Dr. Hoyt of all the money he needed for his various institutions, he was as unconcerned as is a little child holding its mother's hand. There were no lines upon his brow, there was no shadow of anxiety upon his face, only the large, good-natured English smile. Yet there were five hundred orphans to feed, widows to be maintained in the almshouses, professors' fees to be paid in his college, and students to house and sometimes clothe. Spurgeon's attitude was: "The Lord is a good banker, and I trust Him. He has never failed me. Why should I be anxious?"[1]

Hoyt also stated that Spurgeon stood out as a leader because of his "spiritual expectancy." The same biographical source went on to say this:

As an outcome of his . . . childlike credulity Spurgeon always expected spiritual results from his preaching. He expected conversions from both his spoken and printed sermons, and he chided any student of his that did not expect results every time he preached! "According to your faith it shall be done unto you" was Spurgeon's motto text. He went into the pulpit "forecasting victory, not foreboding defeat." He expected to vanquish and not to be vanquished. In the same way he summoned his great church to special prayer for those who were ill and expected that they would recover because of "the prayer of faith." Every recovery was hailed jubilantly as another evidence that God will listen to his children when they cry to him.[2]

Spurgeon's childlike credulity and spiritual expectancy had their origin in the same trait: his steadfast faith in God. In every area of his ministry, Spurgeon exhibited an extraordinary confidence that God would equip, enable, and provide. And he believed this confidence could be applied to every matter in a Christian's life—not just those issues related to the spiritual realm. He taught that we ought to have a complete trust in God for all things, and that we ought to entrust all things to God. In one sermon he said,

∞

*You believe in God for your soul. Believe in him about your property. Believe in God about your sick wife or your dying child. Believe in God about your losses and bad debts and declining business.*[3]

∞

That may seem a bold statement, as if we could demand from God that every negative circumstance have a positive outcome. But Spurgeon wasn't implying that God is some sort of cosmic genie who is at our disposal to grant our every wish. Rather, his point was that in everything, no matter what the potential outcome, we are to trust God rather than human reason or strength. He couldn't have stated it more simply than this: "Faith is reason at rest with God."[4]

Faith looks to God as holding the answer. It sets aside our finite knowledge and rests on His infinite wisdom, which He reveals to us in Scripture. As Spurgeon noted: "Our faith deals with what God says, not with what learned men think."[5]

## –Casting Oneself Upon God's Promises–

How do we demonstrate our faith in God? Spurgeon put it this way: "The pith, the essence of faith, lies in this—a casting oneself on the promise."[6]

Spurgeon could just as well have said "a casting oneself on God." As we consider a promise from God—any promise—we would do well to remember the character of the One behind that promise. For example, God is true, perfect, unchanging, reliable, loving, just, and faithful. And we can know with absolute certainty that His promises are consistent with His character. So if we ever doubt one of God's promises, we are, in essence, doubting one or more aspects of God's own character. We are doubting His truthfulness, His perfection, His immutability, His reliability, His love, His justice, and His faithfulness, or some other aspect of Him.

What's more, the incredible number of promises that abound in Scripture ought to help us realize the extent of God's care for us. Spurgeon's book *The Check Book of the Bank of Faith* has 366 daily devotions, and every single one looks at promises found in the Bible. We have so many promises at our disposal that we can safely assume nothing will ever happen to us that falls outside of God's providential ability to care for us. And the greatest assurance of all is that God keeps His promises. In the preface of *The Check Book of the Bank of Faith*, Spurgeon wrote: "God has given no pledge which He will not redeem, and encouraged no hope which He will not fulfill."[7]

A little later in the preface he added:

∞

*My brethren, God is good. He will not forsake you: He will bear you through. There is a promise prepared for your present emergencies; and if you will believe and plead it at the mercy-seat through Jesus Christ, you shall see the hand of the Lord stretched out to help you. Everything else will fail, but His word never will. He has been to me so faithful in countless instances that I must encourage you to trust Him.*[8]

∞

Of course, our ability to cast ourselves upon God's promises is dependent upon knowing what those promises are, which requires a familiarity with His Word. The more intimately we know the Scriptures, the greater the security we will experience in the Christian life, for it is our awareness of God's promises that informs us of the many ways He stands ready to help us.

Simply put, exercising faith in God means trusting Him. And when it comes to trusting God with our work of ministry, this was Spurgeon's attitude: "I make bold to assert that, in the service of God, nothing is impossible, and nothing is improbable. Go in for great things, brethren, in the name of God; risk everything on His promise, and according to your faith shall it be done unto you."[9]

Again, we should not take this to mean that God will grant our every desire. Our trust in God needs to be in harmony with the principles and pledges He has given to us in the Bible. To "go in for great things . . . in the name of God" is to pursue that which is consistent with God's character, honors Him, and matches up with His will.

## —THE CHALLENGE OF FAITH—

While the matter of placing our faith in God may sound easy, Spurgeon acknowledged that trusting God can actually be difficult: "Faith is hard because it is easy. It is difficult because there is no difficulty in it. And it seems obscure simply because it is so clear."[10]

Perhaps that is why, in most matters in life, our first inclination is to "take care of it ourselves." We move ahead with what we think are the obvious solutions, and in doing so, we put our faith in human achievement rather than divine accomplishment. Our bent is to be independent, whereas God longs for us to be dependent. "We generally make our worst blunders,"

Spurgeon wrote, "about things that are perfectly easy, when the thing is so plain that we do not ask God to guide us, because we think our own common sense will be sufficient, and so we commit grave errors."[11]

Thus Spurgeon wrote that in every circumstance, no matter how small or simple, the principle we need to keep in mind is this: "Dependence upon God is the flowing fountain of success."[12]

Are you trusting God not only with the bigger decisions and responsibilities you face, but the smaller ones as well? Do you invite God's participation in literally every area of your life and ministry? Do you ask Him to guide you not only when you teach or give counsel or organize plans, but also when you greet others at church, talk on the telephone, or carry out what might seem an insignificant activity?

Spurgeon knew success in his ministry because of his persistent dependence upon God—a dependence that could be clearly seen by those around him. In the previous chapter, we observed Spurgeon's comment, "I always feel it well just to put a few words of prayer between everything I do." We can be sure that in those prayers, he was casting himself upon God, expressing his faith and dependence upon the Almighty. Does the way in which we carry out our leadership—and all the other responsibilities of our lives—reveal to others a clear dependence upon God in everything? Are they seeing an example that inspires them to do likewise?

## Our Faith and Our Usefulness to God

Spurgeon pointed out that our success in the Lord's work is determined not by our ability or our zeal, but by the amount of faith we have in God. In an address to church leaders he said,

∞

*Our work especially requires faith. If we fail in faith, we had better not have undertaken it; and unless we obtain faith commensurate with the service, we shall soon grow weary of it. It is proven by all observation that success in the Lord's service is very generally in proportion to faith. It certainly is not in proportion to ability, nor does it always run parallel with a display of zeal; but it is invariably according to the measure of faith, for this is a law of the Kingdom without exception, "According to your faith be it unto you." It is essential, then, that we should have faith if we are to be useful, and that we should have great faith if we are to be greatly useful.*[13]

∞

The great men and women of the Bible accomplished great things because they were men and women of great faith. And it is only with faith that we can expect to make real progress and advance the front lines of God's kingdom. Spurgeon said, "Faith is our battle-ax and weapon of war; woe to the warrior who forgets it!"[14]

When we as ministry leaders exhibit strong faith in God, we increase our usefulness to Him in multiple ways—one being that the Lord can use our example to encourage others toward greater faith. The apostle Paul, while in jail and uncertain about his future, wrote, "I can do *all* things through Christ who strengthens me" and, "My God shall supply *all your need* according to His riches in glory by Christ Jesus" (Philippians 4:13, 19, italics added). Countless Christians through the ages have been uplifted toward stronger faith through those words. We should desire that our faith, as revealed through our words and actions, is similarly uplifting to others.

## –THE BENEFITS OF EXERCISING FAITH–

Each year, the Pastors' College founded by Spurgeon hosted a conference for pastors and church leaders. The conferences were held at the Metropolitan Tabernacle, and the highlight of these meetings was Spurgeon's presidential address. In his 1872 address, Spurgeon asked, "What does our faith work in us?" Here are three key benefits he mentioned, among others:

∞

*It works in us, first,* a glorious independence of man. *We are glad of earnest helpers, but we can do without them. We are grateful for our good deacons, but we dare not make flesh our arm. We are very glad if God raises up brethren in other churches who* will fraternize with us, but we do not lean upon them. The man who believes in God, and believes in Christ, and believes in the Holy Ghost, will stay himself upon the Lord alone. . . . God alone is sufficient for us, and in His might we shall achieve the purpose of our being. . . .

True faith in God will also make us abundant in good works. The eleventh of Hebrews is a chapter dedicated to the glorification of faith; but if I assert that it records the good works of the saints, can anybody contradict me? Is it not as much a record of works as of faith? Ay, verily, because where there is much faith, there shall surely ere long be abundant good works. I have no notion of that faith which does not produce good works, especially in the preacher. . . . [15]

Faith in God enables many of you, I know right well, to bear much hardship, and exercise much self-denial, and yet to persevere in your ministry. . . . True faith makes a man feel that it is sweet to be a living sacrifice unto God.

Only faith could keep us in the ministry, for ours is not a vocation which brings with it golden pay; it is not a calling which men would follow who desire honor and rank. We have all kinds of evils to

*endure, evils as numerous as those which Paul*
*included in his famous catalogue of trials.*[16]

∽

Spurgeon's comments in that last paragraph are particularly noteworthy, for he was well acquainted with hardships and trials, which are part and parcel of the terrain of leadership. That all Christians will face difficulties in life is assumed in Scripture; the apostle James wrote, "Consider it all joy, my brethren, when you encounter various trials" (1:2 NASB). He went on to say that "the testing of your *faith* produces *endurance*" (verse 3, italics added). If we who are leaders are expected to manifest strong faith and walk a steadfast course, then we should not express surprise that our portion of trials in life will be greater, for only then will we possess the resolve that's commensurate to the responsibilities we are called to bear upon our shoulders. With that in mind, let's consider the perspective we ought to have when it comes to trials.

## –TRIALS AS STEPPING-STONES TO GREATER THINGS–

Spurgeon said it is faith that enables us to see our hardships as "stepping-stones to grander results" and "platforms for the display of His grace," as he put it:

∞

*Faith leads us to believe in difficulties being overruled to promote success. Because we believe in God, and in His Holy Spirit, we believe that difficulties will be greatly sanctified to us, and that they are only placed before us as stepping-stones to grander results. We believe in defeats, my brethren; we believe in going back with the banner trailed in the mire, persuaded that this may be the surest way to lasting triumph. We believe in waiting, weeping, and agonizing; we believe in a non-success which prepares us for doing greater and higher work, for which we should not have been fitted unless anguish had sharpened our soul. We believe in our infirmities, and even glory in them; we thank God that we are not so eloquent as we could wish to be, and have not all the abilities we might desire, because now we know that "the excellency of the power" shall "be of God, and not of us." Faith enables us so to rejoice in the Lord that our infirmities become platforms for the display of His grace.*[17]

∞

Indeed, faith enables us to see the silver lining in the clouds when it comes to the setbacks of life. As Spurgeon said, we should fully expect times of defeat, weeping, and agonizing—all of which work to forge in us a greater dependence upon God and a more enduring faith:

∞

*God never gives strong faith without fiery trial; He will not build a strong ship without subjecting it to very mighty storms; He will not make you a mighty warrior if He does not intend to try your skill in battle. The sword of the Lord must be used; the blades of heaven must be smitten against the armour of the evil one, and yet they shall not break, for they are of true Jerusalem metal which shall never snap. We shall conquer, if we begin the battle in the right way. If we have sharpened our swords on the cross, we have nothing whatever to fear; for though we may be sometimes cast down and discomfited, we shall assuredly at last put to flight all our adversaries, for we are the sons of God even now. Why, then, should we fear? Who shall bid us "stay," if God bid us advance?[18]*

∞

Spurgeon spoke those words from intimate experience; he faced numerous fiery trials in his own life. For example, he suffered poor health through most of his years of ministry, enduring agonizingly severe attacks of rheumatic gout that often left him bedridden and depressed. Susannah, his wife, had a condition that left her semi-invalid for long periods of time. Spurgeon's love for her grew deeper through it all, yet it pained him terribly to see her in such a state. And because Spurgeon was not a college-educated minister and was not ordained, the London newspapers made him out to be a charlatan and roundly criticized him.

In spite of these hardships and many others, Spurgeon was able to say, "I have never lost my calm faith in God, but at times I have been so depressed that the cable has been strained to the utmost."[19]

And should we ever find ourselves at the point where "the cable has been strained to the utmost," we can rest in knowing that God will never give us more than we can bear (see 1 Corinthians 10:13). Thus Spurgeon declared:

∞

*It is well to learn that God doth not put heavy burdens upon weak shoulders, and He doth not allot ordeals fit only for full-grown men to those who are but babes. He educates our faith, testing it by trials which increase little by little in proportion as our faith has increased. He only expects us to do man's work and to endure man's afflictions, when we have passed through the childhood state, and have arrived at the stature of men in Christ Jesus. Expect, then, beloved, your trials to multiply as you proceed towards heaven. Do not think that as you grow in grace the path will become smoother beneath your*

*feet, and the heavens serener above your heads. On
the contrary, reckon that as God gives you greater
skill as a soldier, He will send you upon more ardu-
ous enterprises; and as He more fully fits your
barque to brave the tempest and the storm, so will
He send you out upon more boisterous seas, and
upon longer voyages, that you may honour him, and
still further increase in holy confidence.*[20]

∞

While trials often leave us feeling disillusioned, there's great
comfort in knowing that the end result is growth in holy
confidence and greater skill as a soldier of the Lord.

Now, is it ever possible for us to grow so much in faith that we
become immune to the debilitating effects of trials? Spurgeon
asked and responded to that very question:

∞

*Can a man's faith grow so strong that he will never
afterwards doubt at all? I reply, no. He who has
the strongest faith will have sorrowful intervals of
despondency. I suppose there has scarcely ever been
a Christian who has not, at some time or other, had
the most painful doubts concerning his acceptance in
the Beloved. All God's children will have paroxysms
of doubt even though they be usually strong in faith.*[21]

∞

Rather than attempt to circumvent life's difficulties or avoid them altogether, we should persevere through them and let them work their purifying effects in us.

## –The Connection Between Prayer and Faith–

When problems arise, then, our first instinct should be to cast ourselves upon God and His promises. And prayer is an essential part of making that happen. Spurgeon says:

∞

*How, then, are we to cast our care upon God? Two things need to be done. It is a heavy load that is to be cast upon God, and it requires the hand of prayer and the hand of faith to make the transfer. Prayer tells God what the care is, and asks God to help, while faith believes that God can and will do it. Prayer spreads the letter of trouble and grief before the Lord, and opens [each ailment's full] budget, and then faith cries, "I believe that God cares, and cares for me; I believe that He will bring me out of my distress, and make it promote His own glory."* [22]

∞

That there is a connection between faith and prayer shouldn't surprise us. As we learned in the previous chapter, Spurgeon was a man of unceasing prayer. If it is prayer that opens the channel for us to express our faith in God's care, then Spurgeon, because he was a man of habitual prayer, paved the way for himself to become a man of habitual faith.

Prayer, then, is our starting point. And upon placing the matter in God's hand, faith says, "Father, I trust You . . . completely. I know You are working in my life and through these circumstances for my good and Your glory."

Our goal, then, should be to see everything in life—*everything*—as an opportunity to deepen and broaden our faith in God. After all, as Spurgeon quaintly pointed out, "No man was ever yet found guilty of believing in God too much."[23]

## –THE REWARD OF THE FAITHFUL–

Strong faith has many desirable results. It bears fruit all around us, as well as within us. It glorifies God, putting His grace, wisdom, and strength on display before a watching world. It enables us to endure the difficulties we are guaranteed to encounter all through life here on earth—and those very difficulties, in turn, serve to instill within us an even stronger faith.

But that's not all. The best is still yet to come. As the parable of the talents indicates, God is generous when it comes to rewarding His workers. The level of diligence we invest in our service to the Lord here on earth will have a proportionally greater payoff in eternity. "The reward of all faithful stewards is exceedingly great: let us aspire to it," Spurgeon said. "The Lord will make the man who was faithful in a few things to be ruler over many things."[24]

Yes, cultivating a childlike credulity—a simple faith that endures—will, at times, find you "strained to the utmost." And as you continue to mature, you can expect that you'll find yourself sent out "upon more boisterous seas, and upon longer voyages, that you may honour him." But in the end, it will be well worthwhile. For as Spurgeon noted, "It will be seven heavens in one to hear our Master say, 'Well done, good and faithful servant.'"[25]

# SPURGEON with His Pen

FROM DAY TO DAY and from year to year my faith believes in the wisdom and love of God, and I know that I shall not believe in vain. No good word of His has ever failed, and I am sure that none shall ever fall to the ground.

I put myself into His hand for guidance. I know not the way that I should choose: the Lord shall choose mine inheritance for me. I need counsel and advice; for my duties are intricate, and my condition is involved. I seek to the Lord, as the High Priest of old looked to his Urim and Thummim. The counsel of the infallible God I seek in preference to my own judgment or the advice of friends. Glorious Jehovah, Thou shalt guide me!

Soon the end will come: a few more years, and I must depart out of this world unto the Father. My Lord will be near my bed. He will meet me at heaven's gate: He will welcome me to the glory-land. I shall not be a stranger in heaven: my own God and Father will receive me to its endless bliss. Glory be to Him who will guide me here, and receive me hereafter. Amen.[26]

# ᴬ Commitment *to* Holiness

> "As He who called you is holy, you also be holy in all your conduct, because it is written, 'Be holy, for I am holy.'"
>
> —1 Peter 1:15–16

In the same way that the tallest trees and other projectiles on a landscape tend to attract lightning, so did Spurgeon's prominence draw more than his share of detractors and critics. His success in ministry and his exemplary life led some to raise questions about his motives and elicit suspicions that surely he wasn't as good a man as he appeared to be. One reason skepticism arose so easily is that hypocrisy was a common problem in the pulpits of that day; moral weakness in a minister's life was more the norm than the exception.

Yet Spurgeon had nothing to hide. In fact, near the end of his life, someone wrote a letter threatening to expose him in some way. Spurgeon responded, "You may write my life across the sky; I have nothing to conceal."[1]

Spurgeon's exhortations for Christians to live holy lives were not mere lip service. Rather, they emanated from a deeply heartfelt conviction of the absolute necessity for holiness in his own life as a messenger of no less than God Himself. So passionately did he feel about this that he said, "Every saint must be holy, but he should be holiest of all who ministers before the Lord."[2] He recognized that the works of a holy God are impaired when transmitted through an unholy vessel:

∞

*You all know the injurious effects frequently produced upon water through flowing along leaden pipes, even so the gospel itself, in flowing through men who are spiritually unhealthy, may be debased until it grows injurious to their hearers.*[3]

*Let the channel through which the living water is to flow be both clear and clean.*[4]

∞

Our effectiveness, then, is proportionate to our holiness. As Spurgeon said,

∞

*We must cultivate the highest degree of godliness because our work imperatively requires it. The labor of the Christian ministry is well performed in exact proportion to the vigor of our renewed nature. Our work is only well done when it is well with ourselves. As is the workman, such will the work be.*[5]

∞

## –THE REQUIREMENT FOR HOLINESS–

Scripture clearly sets the standard when it says an overseer "must be above reproach" and "must have a good reputation with those outside the church" (1 Timothy 3:2, 7 NASB). Elsewhere we read that leaders are to "shepherd the flock of God . . . being examples to the flock" (1 Peter 5:2–3). The apostle Paul, while training Timothy for ministry leadership, told Timothy to "be an example to the believers in word, in conduct, in love, in spirit, in faith, in purity" (1 Timothy 4:12). After all, how can we expect people to know and understand the holiness God desires in a Christian's life unless they see it on display in us? We ought to live in such a way that we can say, with the apostle Paul, "Imitate me, just as I also imitate Christ" (1 Corinthians 11:1).

## –AN AWARENESS THAT
## OTHERS ARE WATCHING–

As we carry on our work of ministry, it's essential we live with a constant awareness that people are watching us. We have the potential to be either a positive or negative influence upon others. We are accountable for the spiritual well-being of our followers, and need to exercise care that our thoughts, words, and actions represent God and the Christian life accurately.

"Our lives should be such as men may safely copy," Spurgeon once summarized.[6] This was a recurring theme in the messages Spurgeon gave at the Pastors' College and the annual college conferences:

∞

*A very considerable and essential part of Christian ministry lies in example. Our people take much note of what we say out of the pulpit, and what we do in the social circle and elsewhere. Do you find it easy, my brethren, to be saints?—such saints that others may regard you as examples? We ought to be such husbands that every husband in the parish may safely be such as we are. Is it so? We ought to be the best of fathers.[7]*

*It is a shocking state of things when good people say, "Our minister undoes in the parlor what he has done in the pulpit; he preaches very well, but his life does not agree with his sermons." Our Lord Jesus would have us perfect even as our Father who is in heaven is perfect. Every Christian should be holy; but we are laid under a sevenfold obligation to it: how can we expect the Divine blessing if it be not so?*[8]

*We are watched by a thousand eagle eyes; let us so act that we shall never need to care if all heaven, and earth, and hell, swelled the list of spectators. Our public position is a great gain if we are enabled to exhibit the fruits of the Spirit in our lives; take heed, brethren, that you throw not away the advantage.*[9]

∞

## −THE SERIOUSNESS OF SIN−

One of the more common reasons Christians in general succumb to temptation is that they rationalize, "One little sin won't hurt." Ministry leaders are no less susceptible to such reasoning. We say, "Just this one time; I won't do it again." Or, "This won't hurt anyone." Yet Spurgeon had the right perspective when he said:

∞

*You cannot, though you may think you can, pre-serve a moderation in sin. If you commit one sin, it is like the melting of the lower glacier upon the Alps; the others must follow in time.*[10]

*Little sins are like little thieves, they open the door to big ones.*[11]

*A loose stone here, and a fallen tie there, and a rotting timber in a third place, will soon bring on a total ruin to a tenement, but the hand of diligence maintains the fabric. Thus we must watch our spiritual house, lest we fall by little and little.*[12]

*One pampered sin will slay the soul as surely as one dose of poison will kill the body.*[13]

∞

Satan takes a special delight in the failure of a spiritual leader. He knows that to seduce just one leader into sin can have a ripple effect that disrupts the lives of everyone under that leader's influence. Thus he is especially persistent in his assaults against those in key positions of ministry, and we need to stand ever vigilant because his schemes are so crafty and subtle. As Spurgeon noted in his *Lectures to My Students*:

∞

*The great enemy of souls takes care to leave no stone unturned for the preacher's ruin.*[14]

*Take heed, therefore, brethren, for the enemy hath a special eye upon you. You shall have his most subtle insinuations, and incessant solicitations, and violent assaults. As wise and learned as you are, take heed to yourselves lest he overwit you. The devil is a greater scholar than you, and a nimbler disputant; he can "transform himself into an angel of light" to deceive, he will get within you and trip up your heels before you are aware; he will play the juggler with you undiscerned, and cheat you of your faith or innocency, and you shall not know that you have lost it: nay, he will make you believe it is multiplied or increased when it is lost. You shall see neither hook nor line, much less the subtle angler himself, while he is offering you his bait. And his baits shall be so fitted to your temper and disposition, that he will be sure to find advantages within you, and make your own principles and inclinations to betray you; and whenever he ruineth you, he will make you the instrument of your own ruin. Oh, what a conquest will he think he hath got, if he can make a minister lazy and unfaithful; if he can tempt a minister into covetousness or scandal! He will glory against the church, and say, "These are your holy preachers: you see what their preciseness is, and whither it will bring them." He will glory against Jesus Christ Himself,*

*and say, "These are thy champions! I can make thy
chiefest servants to abuse thee; I can make the stewards of thy house unfaithful."*[15]

∞

## –SIN'S IMPACT ON OUR MINISTRY–

No matter how much we might try to convince ourselves that
a secret sin won't hurt others or that we can quarantine its
effects upon our spiritual service, the reality is that every sin—
no matter how small or private—is a gangrene that deadens
our effectiveness in ministry. No amount of mental, emotional,
or physical effort on our part can change the fact that sin is
a *spiritual* problem that has definite repercussions on *all* areas
of our spiritual life, leading to a loss of spiritual power
and usefulness.

∞

*Your whole life, your whole pastoral life especially,
will be affected by the vigor of your piety. If your zeal
grows dull, you will not pray well in the pulpit; you
will pray worse in the family, and worst in the study
alone. When your soul becomes lean, your hearers,
without knowing how or why, will find that your
prayers in public have little savor for them; they will
feel your barrenness, perhaps, before you perceive
it yourself. Your discourses will next betray your
declension. You may utter as well-chosen words, and*

*as fitly-ordered sentences, as aforetime; but there will be a perceptible loss of spiritual force.*[16]

∞

Spurgeon also pointed out that spiritual leaders are like public clocks by which onlookers set their watches and, when a leader is in error, he is responsible for leading others into that same error:

∞

*[If the] Greenwich Observatory should go amiss, half London would lose its reckoning. So is it with the minister; he is the parish-clock, many take their time from him, and if he be incorrect, then they all go wrongly, more or less, and he is in a great measure accountable for all the sin which he occasions.*[17]

*The members of our congregation gather lessons from what we do as well as from what we say, and this should make us very careful lest we lead them astray. Be holy, that others may be holy.*[18]

∞

Given the great degree to which sin can impair God's ability to use us, Spurgeon makes this plea:

∞

*If there is anything we are doing, or leaving undone, any evil we are harbouring, or any grace we are*

*neglecting, which may make us unfit to be used of
God, let us pray the Lord to cleanse, and mend, and
scour us till we are vessels fit for the Master's use.
. . . Let us not be content till we are useful, but make
this the main design and ambition of our lives.*[19]

∞

## −PREVENTING UNHOLINESS−

There's more to maintaining holiness than simply avoiding
sin. Rather than wait for temptation to strike and react
accordingly, we can take proactive measures to nurture holiness in our lives. "They tell me there is as much of a tree
under as above ground," Spurgeon said, "and certainly it is
so with a believer; his visible life would soon wither if not for
his secret life."[20]

What can we do in secret to nurture our holiness so that our
public lives won't wither? First and foremost is a complete
dependence upon the Holy Spirit:

∞

*Evermore, in beginning, in continuing, and in end-
ing any and every good work, [we must] consciously
and in very truth depend upon the Holy Ghost. Even
a sense of your need of Him He must give you; and
the prayers with which you entreat Him to come
must come from Him. You are engaged in a work*

*so spiritual, so far above all human power, that to
forget the Spirit is to ensure defeat. . . . Render Him
homage by yielding yourself to His impulses, and by
hating everything that grieves Him.*[21]

∽

The Bible says that when you "walk in the Spirit . . . you shall
not fulfill the lust of the flesh" (Galatians 5:16), thus affirming
that a deliberate choice to walk in the Spirit's ways is an anti-
dote to sin.

Another essential to cultivating our secret inner person is
closeness with God:

∽

*We must, dear friends, never become weak in
another sense, namely, in our communion with God.
David slackened his fellowship with God, and Satan
vanquished him through Bathsheba; Peter followed
afar off, and soon denied his Lord. Communion with
God is the right arm of our strength; and if this be
broken, we are weak as water. Without God, we can
do nothing; and in proportion as we attempt to live
without Him, we ruin ourselves. . . . If it be true that
only as we hang upon the Lord are we strong, then
broken fellowship will soon bring broken strength.*[22]

∽

As we walk in the Spirit and stay in close communion with God, our minds are more likely to stay focused upon the things of the Lord, which can also help us in our desire to live holy lives. Thus Spurgeon advised, "Preoccupation of mind is a great safeguard from temptation. Fill a bushel with corn and you will keep out the chaff."[23]

We who are in ministry leadership can also find strength in numbers. How often have we been encouraged by the strength and resolve of a fellow worker who practices personal purity? For the times when we're discouraged or sorely tempted, having such a friend or two to lean upon can make a big difference:

∞

*An old Puritan has well observed that "Nothing in all the world contributes so much to the kindling, the firing, and the inflaming of men's hearts after holiness, as the society of those that are holy."*[24]

*The mountain of life must be scaled; crevasses, chasms, precipices, must be encountered. Almost without exception we must be roped together in this mountaineering: let the wise man accept only as his partners those who will pursue the ways of faith and virtue, for with these only will he reach the summit.*[25]

∞

## –THE BENEFITS OF HOLINESS–

At times we will find it a struggle to live holy—sometimes so much so that we may even wonder if the only "way out" is to succumb to the temptation—then ask God for forgiveness. But we know all too well that the supposed relief that comes from such indulgence is short-lived . . . only to be quickly followed by the Spirit's piercing sword of conviction. Moreover, to surrender in such a fashion is to intentionally abuse God's grace. No, we don't have to give in. "God is faithful, who will not allow you to be tempted beyond what you are able, but with the temptation will also make the way of escape, that you may be able to bear it" (1 Corinthians 10:13). What's more, the relief we gain from persevering on the path of holiness is real and lasting. Consider these benefits that Spurgeon noted:

∞

*Sanctity in ministers is a loud call to sinners to repent, and when allied with holy cheerfulness it becomes wondrously attractive.*[26]

*In holiness God is more clearly seen than in anything else.*[27]

*The serene, silent beauty of a holy life is the most powerful influence in the world, next to the might of the Spirit of God.*[28]

*Only sanctified souls are satisfied souls.*[29]

∞

An additional benefit observed by Spurgeon is that holiness, because it is so supremely important, can make up for certain deficiencies we might have:

∞

*You must have holiness; and, dear brethren, if you should fail in mental qualifications (though I hope you will not), and if you should have a slender measure of the oratorical faculty (though I trust you will not), yet, depend upon it, a holy life is, in itself, a wonderful power, and will make up for many deficiencies; it is, in fact, the best sermon the best man can ever deliver.*[30]

∞

## −AN ONGOING PURSUIT−

As pointed out earlier, it's easy to rationalize that small or infrequent lapses into sin surely cannot be all that harmful. Yet the command of Scripture is blunt: "As He who called you is holy, you also be holy in *all* your conduct" (1 Peter 1:15, italics added). Spurgeon put it eloquently in the following quotations:

∞

*Much of the beauty of holiness lies in little things. Microscopic holiness is the perfection of excellence: if a life will bear examination in each hour of it, it is pure indeed. Those who are not careful about their words, and even their thoughts, will soon grow careless concerning their more notable actions. Those who tolerate sin in what they think to be little things, will soon indulge it in greater matters. To live by the day and to watch each step, is the true pilgrimage method. More lies in the careful noting of every single act than careless minds can well imagine.*[31]

*Holiness is no blazing comet, amazing nations with a transient glory; it is a fixed star that, with still, calm radiance, shines on through the darkness of a corrupt age. Holiness is persevering obedience; it is not holiness at all if it be occasional zeal and sensational piety.*[32]

*Godliness is a life-long business.*[33]

∞

## –Our Reason for Holy Living–

Above all, it helps to remember why holiness is so important. As spiritual leaders, we are not our own. We were bought with a price, and we are ambassadors of God to a watching world—

ambassadors of not just any earthly king, but the King of all kings and Lord of all lords:

∞

*Behave yourselves, Christian brethren, for you bear a great Name. . . . If you are indeed in Christ's stead, what manner of persons ought you to be! May God help you to be worthy of the embassage on which you are sent!* [34]

*Be ye holy, for ye serve a holy God. If you were making a present to a prince, you would not find Him a lame horse to ride upon; you would not offer Him a book out of which leaves had been torn, nor carry Him a timepiece whose wheels were broken. No, the best of the best you would give to one whom you honored and loved. Give your very best to your Lord. Seek to be at your best whenever you serve Him.* [35]

∞

Indeed, Spurgeon pursued purity with a passion. When it came to holiness, he lived what he preached. He constantly admonished other leaders toward a similar commitment in their own lives for the simple reason that the Bible calls for such. And he was ever mindful of the impact a holy life can have on a multitude of others. One evening during a lecture to his pastoral students Spurgeon quoted Robert

Murray McCheyne, a devout Scottish preacher whose words capture well the truth that the call to a holy life is a truly noble calling indeed:

> Remember you are God's sword, His instrument—I trust, a chosen vessel unto Him to bear His name. In great measure, according to the purity and perfection of the instrument, will be the success. It is not great talents God blesses so much as likeness to Jesus. A holy minister is an awful weapon in the hand of God.[36]

# SPURGEON on His Knees

OUR FATHER . . . we adore Thee because Thou art holy, and we love Thee for Thine infinite perfection. For now we sigh and cry after holiness ourselves. Sanctify us wholly, spirit, soul and body. Lord, we mourn over the sins of our past life and our present shortcomings. We bless Thee [that] Thou hast forgiven us; we are reconciled to Thee by the death of Thy Son. . . .

Lord, purify us in head, heart and hand; and if it be needful that we should be put into the fire to be refined as silver is refined, we would even welcome the fire if we may be rid of the dross. Lord, save us from constitutional sin, from sins of temperament, from sins of our surroundings. Save us from ourselves in every shape, and grant us especially to have the light of love strong within us. . . .

Lord, help Thy poor children to be holy. Oh! keep us so if we are so; keep us even from stumbling, and present us faultless before Thy presence at last.[37]

# ᴬ Heart
## *for*
# Service

"IN LOWLINESS OF MIND LET

EACH ESTEEM OTHERS BETTER

THAN HIMSELF."

—PHILIPPIANS 2:3

Considering the magnitude of Charles Spurgeon's ministry and fame, it would have been very easy for him to become even marginally prideful about his accomplishments and assume an air of superiority over others. Yet no matter how much Spurgeon's successes and prominence continued to mount, he always wore the mantle of a servant, maintaining a humility uncharacteristic of someone of his stature.

Spurgeon's heart for serving others—even his own brother—dated back to his childhood, as evidenced by this amusing account he shared in his autobiography:

∞

*Long after my own sons had grown to manhood, I recalled to my father's recollection an experience of which, until then, he had never had an explanation. My brother, as a child, suffered from weak ankles, and in consequence frequently fell down, and so got into trouble at home. At last, hoping to cure him of what father thought was only carelessness, he was threatened that he should be whipped every time he came back showing any signs of having fallen down. When I reminded father of this regulation, he said quite triumphantly, "Yes, it was so, and he was completely cured from that time." "Ah!" I answered, "so you thought, yet it was not so, for he had many a tumble afterwards; but I always managed to wash his knees, and to brush his clothes, so as to remove all traces of his falls."[1]*

∞

At a celebration commemorating Spurgeon's fiftieth birthday, the great Lord Shaftesbury, a popular and influential social and industrial reformer in England and a friend, remarked of Spurgeon, "He began his ministry when only nineteen, and see him now going on as he began. He has not been puffed up by success, but humbled and animated the more to go on in his noble career of good which God in His merciful providence had marked out for him, and for the benefits of mankind."[2]

And after Spurgeon's death, Deacon T. H. Olney, who was instrumental in bringing Spurgeon to London and worked alongside him for nearly forty years, gave this tribute: "He was first of all a man of faith, a man of humble trust. He retained much of the child in his nature. God was his Father, and his trust was as simple and childlike at the end of his career as it was at the beginning."[3]

Spurgeon was critical of ministers who lacked the humility and servant attitude that is to characterize all Christians and dreaded that he might ever become prideful himself:

∞

*What a grand set of men some of the preachers of the past age thought themselves to be! . . . The proud divines never shook hands with anybody, except, indeed, with the deacons, and a little knot of evidently superior persons. . . . If ever I should affect the airs of a great man, and set myself up above you all, and by proud manners cease to have sympathy with you, I hope the Lord will speedily take me down, and make me right in spirit again.*[4]

∞

He also shared frequently his convictions about the necessity of having a servant's heart. He could not have been more direct when he said, early in his ministry, "The very motto of a Christian should be, 'I serve.'"[5] And many years later, in another sermon, he said,

❧

*As long as there is breath in our bodies, let us serve Christ. As long as we can think, as long as we can speak, as long as we can work, let us serve Him. Let us even serve Him with our last gasp.*[6]

❧

## —Every Leader a Servant—

Spurgeon didn't see church leaders as exempt from the call to servanthood. If anything, he felt ministers should be more selfless than their brethren. He stressed that leaders were to serve alongside their followers, citing no less than the great Roman emperor Caesar as an example:

❧

*We are to be examples to our flock in all things. In all diligence, in all gentleness, in all humility, and in all holiness we are to excel. When Caesar went on his wars, one thing always helped his soldiers to bear hardships: they knew that Caesar fared as they fared. He marched if they marched, he thirsted if they thirsted, and he was always in the heart of the battle if they were fighting. We must do more than others if we are officers in Christ's army. We must not cry, "Go on," but, "Come on." Our people may justly expect of us, at the very least, that we should be among the most self-denying, the most laborious, and the most earnest in the church, and somewhat more.*[7]

∞

Spurgeon also pointed to the Lord Jesus Christ as an example of a leader who served sacrificially:

∞

*It is heaven to serve Jesus. . . . He is the most magnanimous of captains. There never was His like among the choicest of princes. He is always to be found in the thickest part of the battle. When the wind blows cold He always takes the bleak side of the hill. The heaviest end of the cross lies ever on His shoulders. If He bids us carry a burden, He carries it also. If there is anything gracious, generous, kind, and tender, yea lavish and superabundant in love, you always find it in Him. These forty years and more have I served Him, blessed be His name! and I have had nothing but love from Him. I would be glad to continue yet another forty years in the same dear service here below if so it pleased Him.*[8]

∞

This lines up, of course, with what Jesus said about the purpose of His ministry: That He came not to be served, but to serve

(Mark 10:45). The Lord Himself was not one who lorded His authority over others. And Spurgeon exhorted his fellow leaders to live likewise:

∞

*My brethren, what is our relation to this church? What is our position in it? We are servants. May we always know our place, and keep it! The highest place in the church will always come to the man who willingly chooses the lowest; while he that aspires to be great among his brethren will sink to be least of all. Certain men might have been something if they had not thought themselves so. A consciously great man is an evidently little one. A lord over God's heritage is a base usurper. He that in his heart and soul is always ready to serve the very least of the family; who expects to be put upon; and willingly sacrifices reputation and friendship for Christ's sake, he shall fulfill a heaven-sent ministry. We are not sent to be ministered unto, but to minister.*[9]

∞

## −KEY TRAITS OF A SERVANT−

Numerous biographies about Spurgeon were written in the months after his death, and one characteristic many of them share is an abundance of stories that reveal his big heart for people. While the stories reveal multiple facets of Spurgeon's servant-heartedness, there are certain traits that emerge again and again: selflessness, kindness, humility, helpfulness, and generosity. Let's consider them one by one.

## Selflessness

In response to a generous gift given by over 450 Baptist churches to the Stockwell Orphanage, Spurgeon, who was so overwhelmed he found it hard to speak, said,

∞

*There is no earthly requirement that I myself personally need. God has blessed me with an abundance of everything that wealth can furnish for my own necessities, and therefore I am not hungry after more earthly goods for myself, but I am beyond measure greedy on behalf of God's cause.*[10]

∞

Also in relation to the orphanage, one biographer wrote, "When in financial difficulties about the orphanage, his method always was first to look into his private banking account, and pay over to the funds every penny that he could spare. He next invited his fellow-trustees to do what they could, and not till then did he pray that outside help might be sent."[11]

Spurgeon himself made this statement about the kind of servant God uses:

∽

*The Lord pours most into those who are most empty of self. Those who have least of their own shall have the most of God's. The Lord cares little what the vessel is, whether golden or earthen, so long as it is clean, and disengaged from other uses.*[12]

∽

## Kindness

Spurgeon enjoyed children and was a frequent visitor to the orphanage he had founded with the help of his church and supporters. In the following account we receive yet another glimpse into his heart, which had a soft spot for the less opportune:

> Mr. Charlesworth, the headmaster of the orphanage, said this about how the boys felt toward their president [Spurgeon]: The children loved him, and his visits always called forth the most boisterous demonstrations of delight. His appearance was the signal for a general movement towards the centre of attraction, and he often said, "They compassed me about like bees!" The eagerness with which they sought to grasp his hand often involved the younger children in the risk of being trampled upon by others; but, with ready tact and condescension, he singled out those that were at a disadvantage, and extended them his hand.[13]

The same biographer included a more humorous anecdote illustrating Spurgeon's kindness:

> He was staying at the Hotel des Anglais, at Mentone, when he saw a poor organ-grinder playing in the garden without much success. Pitying him, he took his place at the instrument and ground away. In a few minutes the news went round, and every window was occupied with amused spectators, who threw their money to him lavishly. The organ-grinder went away with the heaviest purse he had possessed for many a day.[14]

Spurgeon's benevolence extended to even the smallest of things. He "was forever giving people something. In the many happy hours that were spent by visitors in Spurgeon's home he would often pluck an 'everlasting flower' that he had taken from his garden to give to the visitor as a memento."[15] On the trait of kindness, Spurgeon himself said,

∞

*If there be one virtue which most commends Christians, it is that of kindness; it is to love the people of God, to love the Church, to love poor sinners, to love all. . . . Imitate Christ in your loving spirits; speak kindly, act kindly, and think kindly, that men may say of you, "He has been with Jesus."*[16]

∞

## Humility

Those who knew Spurgeon best knew his humility was real. It is often said that our true nature reveals itself most in the privacy of our own homes—those who see us at work or church see one side of us, while our family sees quite another. Yet this wasn't the case with Spurgeon. In Charles's autobiography, wife Susannah Spurgeon shared several poignant entries from her husband's personal diary, which dated to his very first days in ministry. This entry is representative of many others like it:

∽

*Lord, keep Thy servant low and humble at Thy feet! How prone am I to pride and vain-glory! Keep me always mindful that I have nothing which I have not received; 'tis grace, free, sovereign grace that has made me to differ. Why should I be chosen an elect vessel? Not that I deserve it, I am sure; but it is rich love.*[17]

∽

In relation to that excerpt and others, Susannah commented:

How marked is his *humility*, even though he must have felt within him the stirrings and throes of the wonderful powers which were afterwards developed. "Forgive me, Lord," he says in one place, "if I have ever had high thoughts of myself,"—so early did the Master implant the precious seeds of that rare grace of meekness, which adorned his after life. After each youthful effort at public exhortation, whether it be engaging in prayer, or addressing Sunday-school children, he seems to be surprised at his own success, and intensely anxious to be kept from pride and self-glory, again and again confessing his own utter weakness, and pleading for God-given strength.[18]

That Susannah penned these words after Charles's death confirms that he retained his humility all through his years of ministry. What's more, Charles and Susannah had twin sons, Charles and Thomas, and after the husband and father passed away, son Charles wrote,

There was one trait in his noble and godly character, which, among many others, always shone with a luster peculiarly its own. His humility was of a Christlike character, and it demands heartiest commendation from those who speak or write about him. Words of eulogy concerning himself were ever painful to him, his motto in this, as in all other matters, being, "not I, but Christ."[19]

That Spurgeon would say, "Not I, but Christ" is consistent with the exhortations he uttered to his students at the Pastors' College:

∞

*Remember that God has come unto us, not to exalt us, but to exalt Himself, and we must see to it that*

*His glory is the one sole object of all we do. He must increase, and I must decrease. Oh, may God bring us to this, and make us walk very carefully and humbly before Him.*[20]

∞

Spurgeon not only encouraged his students toward humility, but reminded them of the one and only source in which they should place their confidence: "It is admirable to see a man humbly conscious of his own weakness, and yet bravely confident in the Lord's power to work through his infirmity."[21]

## Helpfulness

Spurgeon was constantly faced with enormous demands on his time, preaching as many as eight to ten times a week, writing and editing materials for publication, keeping up with an inordinate amount of correspondence, and with the adept help of his brother, James Spurgeon, overseeing the many organizations associated with the Metropolitan Tabernacle. In spite of this schedule, he still made a priority of being available to anyone who wanted personal counsel from him:

> It was his practice to attend at the Tabernacle at three o'clock on Tuesday afternoons for the purpose of private interviews with those who wished to see him, and often before tea-time these would number from thirty to forty. . . . Mr. Spurgeon was generally very happy at the close of an afternoon thus spent, partly because it was always

a joy to help any struggling soul, and also because he usually had several visitors who came to tell how they had received blessing through his sermons. Yet he was entirely free from any feeling of pride in his work, for he attributed the success not to himself, but to the Holy Spirit. On several occasions he remarked . . . that when he came to make close inquiry he found that people who had been helped had received benefit, not through any word of his, but through some text that he had quoted.[22]

Only three months into his ministry in London, the young Spurgeon extended a helping hand to his struggling chapel:

When he first came to London and settled as minister of New Park Street Chapel, the salary offered him was exceedingly small, and it was arranged that he should have the proceeds of the pew rents. In a few weeks' time all the seats in the chapel were let, and the income from this source was greatly increased. Of course it all belonged to the pastor, but at the close of three months he insisted that he should pay for the cleaning and lighting and other incidental expenses, and this arrangement continued for many years.[23]

## Generosity

Spurgeon was also a generous man, giving freely to others, especially those in need. Modern-day biographer Lewis Drummond says this about the gracious minister:

Spurgeon, profoundly committed to the almshouse work, gave himself to it as he did to the Pastors' College and the Stockwell Orphanage. He frequently contributed large sums of his own money for its support. No one ever knew how many bills Spurgeon himself paid for the Home, but he continually settled small accounts for heating, groceries, clothing, and small comforts. On one occasion, at his silver wedding anniversary when he received a [large cash gift], he presented the whole of it as an endowment for the Home. . . . At times, the bills of the Old Ladies Home were paid twice. The officers of the church would pay a bill only to discover that Spurgeon had personally and quietly paid it himself.[24]

W. Y. Fullerton, a close friend of Spurgeon, also mentions the silver wedding anniversary gift and relates the details of another large gift to the minister:

Two of the greatest occasions, apart from the preaching services, were at the silver wedding of pastor and people, and at Mr. Spurgeon's own jubilee. On the first, on May 20, 1879, as the result of a great bazaar, a sum of £6476 was presented to the pastor, the bulk of which he promptly gave as an endowment to the almshouses long connected with the church, and the balance to other good works. The jubilee meetings were held on

June 18 and 19, 1884, and again a presentation was made; this time the sum reached £4500. It would, no doubt, have been considerably more if it had been known that it might have been for the pastor's own use; but people expected that he would give it all away—as he practically did. . . . Literally he gave away a fortune, walking through life from day to day with open heart and open hand."[25]

Spurgeon's generosity was manifest in both big amounts and small, according to Fullerton:

Many a five-pound note was sent to his correspondents when they sought his help in need. During one of his visits to Mentone someone sent him a gift of £5 to help in his expenses. The same day he met a minister who had been ordered there for his health, and knowing something of his circumstances he handed the check to him, saying that his own expenses had already been met. He knew the value of money, and was not careless in the spending of it. . . . He gave with both hands to those in need.[26]

In fact, in one case, Spurgeon "was left a handsome legacy, but when he found there were relatives of the testator in need and unprovided for, he did not accept it."[27]

## Diligence and Wholeheartedness

Two additional characteristics of a true servant, according to Spurgeon, are diligence and wholeheartedness.

Spurgeon exhorted Christian leaders with these reminders about being diligent in their service:

∞

*What kind of men does the Master mean to use? They must be labourers. The man who does not make hard work of his ministry will find it very hard to answer for his idleness at the last great day.*[28]

*Be consumed with love for Christ, and let the flame burn continuously; not flaming up at public meetings, and dying out in the routine work of every day. We need indomitable perseverance, dogged zeal, and a combination of sacred obstinacy, self-denial, holy gentleness, and invincible courage.*[29]

∞

Concerning wholeheartedness in service, Spurgeon told his listeners:

∞

*God deserves to be served with all the energy of which we are capable. If the service of God is worth anything, it is worth everything. We shall find our*

*best reward in the Lord's work if we do it with deter-
mined diligence. Our labor is not in vain in the
Lord, and we know it. Half-hearted work will bring
no reward; but when we throw our whole soul into
the cause, we shall see prosperity.*[30]

*We must never think, because the particular work
we have in hand seems to be insignificant, that
therefore we cannot do it, or should not do it, thoroughly well. We need Divine help to preach aright
to a congregation of one. If a thing is worth doing at
all, it is worth doing well. If you had to sweep a
crossing, it were well to sweep it better than anybody else. . . . Know your work, and bend over it,
throwing your heart and soul into it; for, be it great
or small, you will have to praise God to all eternity
if you are found faithful in it.*[31]

∞

We've looked at several characteristics of a servant's heart—
traits that paint for us a portrait of the kind of person (and
especially leader) whom God can use. Not only did these traits
endear Spurgeon to his family, his ministry peers, and his congregation, but more importantly, they imitated qualities that
are readily found in the Lord Jesus Christ, the master servant.
However, we need to recognize that possessing a servant's

heart doesn't guarantee we will experience the same kind of visible success Spurgeon did. The fact that having a servant's attitude conforms us more to the image of Christ is sufficient reward alone—and should be our greater concern.

## —KEEPING A CLEAR PERSPECTIVE—

Finally, here are three simple guidelines that can make the path of servanthood much smoother for us: be willing to start small, make the best of your mistakes, and give God all the credit.

### Be Willing to Start Small

At a breakfast to men in Aberdeen, Scotland, on March 31, 1861, Spurgeon said,

∞

*Do not think of waiting until you can do some great thing for God; do little things, and then the Master will bid you go up higher. . . . If one wishes to be a steward in God's house, he must first be prepared to serve as a scullion in the kitchen, and be content to wash out the pots and clean the boots. Remember our Lord's rule, "Whosoever exalteth himself shall be abased; and he that humbleth himself shall be exalted."*[32]

∞

## Make the Best of Your Mistakes

Spurgeon knew full well that the road walked by ministry leaders is often rough. From time to time, a decision is made or an action is taken that, later on, in hindsight, we realize wasn't the best course to take. Mistakes will happen; we can be sure of that. But rather than let our setbacks discourage us, we need to view them as opportunities for growth:

∞

*What is the use of regret unless we can rise by it to a better future? Sighs, which do not raise us higher, are an ill use of vital breath. Chasten yourselves, but be not discouraged. Gather up the arrows which aforetime fell wide of the mark, not to break them in passionate despair, but to send them to the target with direct aim, and a more concentrated force. Weave victories out of defeats. Learn success from failure, wisdom from blundering.*[33]

∞

## Give God All the Credit

In a message to the Metropolitan Tabernacle congregation, Spurgeon commented on the extremely rapid growth the church had experienced during the first several years of his pastorate. As he spoke, he made it very clear where the credit was due:

∞

*The greatness of our work compels us to confess that it must be of God, and of God alone. . . . I am always very jealous about this matter; if we do not, as a church and congregation, if we do not, as individuals, always give God the glory, it is impossible that He should continue to work by us.*[34]

∞

Indeed, all that we do as servants is possible only because God empowers us. Consequently, He deserves all the glory and praise for the increase from our ministries. In fact, our service should be rendered such that in everything we do, people see all of God and nothing of us. Spurgeon stated this well on the last New Year's day of his life on earth:

∞

*We would have it so happen that when our life's history is written, whoever reads it will not think of us as self-made men; but as the handiwork of God, in whom His grace is magnified. Not in us may men see the clay, but the Potter's hand. They said of one: "He is a fine preacher"; but of another they said: "We never notice how he preaches, but we always feel that God is great." We wish our whole life to be a sacrifice, an altar of incense continually smoking with perfume to the Most High.*[35]

∞

# SPURGEON
## with His Pen

WE SHALL BE exalted by the Lord if we humble ourselves. For us the way upward is downhill. When we are stripped of self we are clothed with humility, and this is the best of wear. The Lord will exalt us in peace and happiness of mind; He will exalt us into knowledge of His Word and fellowship with Himself; He will exalt us in the enjoyment of sure pardon and justification. The Lord puts His honors upon those who can wear them to the honor of the Giver. He gives usefulness, acceptance, and influence to those who will not be puffed up by them, but will be abased by a sense of greater responsibility. Neither God nor man will care to lift up a man who lifts up himself; but both God and good men unite to honor modest worth.[36]

# A Love for the Lord & His Word

"WITH MY WHOLE HEART I HAVE SOUGHT YOU; OH, LET ME NOT WANDER FROM YOUR COMMANDMENTS!"

—PSALM 119:10

On February 25, 1886, Charles Spurgeon wrote, "I am well, but this gigantic work must crush me sooner or later."[1] A survey of the incredible volume of work Spurgeon did during his ministry years reveals his words to be no exaggeration. Along with pastoring a huge church, he directed several social agencies and outreach ministries, including the Pastors' College, the Stockwell Orphanage, the Old Ladies Home, and the Colportage [literature] Ministry. At the college, he took personal oversight of the selection of the students and lectured to them weekly. Spurgeon also produced and wrote for *The Sword and the Trowel*, a monthly magazine that he began in 1865 and that continued to be published past his death in 1892. He wrote numerous books, and the sermons he preached during his lifetime fill some seventy thick volumes. He was also active in the startup of churches pastored by students from the college, and carried on an immense correspondence.

So great was Spurgeon's output that Charles Ray began his biography of the man with these words: "It is not easy in the compass of a single volume to give anything like a fair idea of Charles Haddon Spurgeon's life and work. Indeed his activities were so manifold, and the channels in which his energies were exerted were so numerous, that the biographer is bewildered by the very mass of material at his disposal."[2]

All the more remarkable is the fact that throughout his life, Spurgeon suffered long and frequent bouts of illness, primarily in relation to his rheumatic gout. At times the pain from his gout was so severe he could not rise out of bed or move about for days or even weeks. A letter Spurgeon wrote to the men's Bible class at the Metropolitan Tabernacle in 1886 hints at how much the pastor's ill health frustrated him:

∞

*Young men, work for the Lord while you can. It would greatly embitter my seasons of painful retirement if I could accuse myself with having wasted the time of my health and strength. When I can work, I pack a mass into a small compass because I am so painfully aware that days and weeks may come wherein I cannot work.*[3]

∞

What was the secret of Spurgeon's enormous productivity? What kept him moving forward in spite of the crushing work-load and debilitating sicknesses? What was the driving force behind it all?

## —AN ALL-CONSUMING LOVE FOR THE LORD—

Spurgeon shared his own answer to a group of pastors at the annual pastors' conference held at the Metropolitan Tabernacle:

∞

*Love to God will help a man to persevere in service when otherwise he would have given up his work. "The love of Christ constraineth us," said one whose heart was all his Master's. I heard one say, the other day, that "the love of Christ ought to constrain us." This is true, but Paul did not so much speak of a duty as of a fact; he said, "the love of Christ constraineth us." Beloved brethren, if you are filled with love to your work, and love to souls, and love to God, you will gladly endure many self-denials, which else would be unbearable.*[4]

∞

Gracing the frontispiece of the first volume of Spurgeon's auto-biography is a photograph of Charles as a young man, which he had given to his wife, Susannah, as a special memento early in their relationship. Susannah treasured this particular photo and wrote, "There have been many representations of my dear husband during the intervening years . . . but I think . . . this early portrait [alone depicts] the intense love and unfailing devotion to his Master which was the secret of his power both with God and man."[5] And in connection with Spurgeon's diary, Susannah noted,

> Perhaps, of greatest price among the precious things which this little book reveals, is the beloved author's personal and intense love to the Lord Jesus. . . . One of the last things he said to me at Mentone, before uncon-sciousness had sealed his dear lips, was this, "O wifie, I have had such a blessed time with my Lord!"[6]

That Spurgeon's devotion to the Lord was intense and unfail-ing was also affirmed by his friend W. Y. Fullerton:

> His soul was seen best when he was listening to some one else speaking the praises of his Lord. He would clasp his hands, catch his breath, the tears would fill his eyes and overflow, his face would shine with a radiance other than of earth, and his rapture would communi-cate itself to those around. . . . At such times you saw the real man, the man to whom the Lord Jesus Christ

was more dear than all the universe, whose boast was in the name of the Lord all the day long.[7]

Biographer J. C. Carlile observed simply, "For Spurgeon, Christ's cross and Christ's presence were the delights of life. He ever loved to point to Christ crucified."[8]

Love is a powerful force indeed. It was love that compelled God to send Jesus Christ to earth to make redemption possible for an utterly wicked and lost mankind. It was love that made Jesus willing to endure an excruciating death on the cross. It was love that inspired God to bless all believers with *every* spiritual blessing in the heavenly places in Christ—riches we do not deserve and could never hope to earn. It is *God's love for us* that led Him to make these sacrifices that are beyond measure, and it is *our love for God* that can enable us to persevere under the most daunting of circumstances. James Douglas wrote that Spurgeon "served much because he loved much. Love oiled the wheels of his activities; gave spontaneity to duty; and made the post of servitude to Christ one of blessed emancipation."[9]

As spiritual leaders, then, we would do well to ask ourselves frequently about the state of our love for the Lord, for it is our love for Him that can help motivate and energize us in all we do. It is our love that will carry us onward when we're ready to quit or we're running on empty. Besides, it is only right that we examine the condition of our love for God in light of the fact that Jesus Himself urged us to "love the Lord your God with all your heart, with all your soul, and with all your mind" (Matthew 22:37).

It's this kind of all-encompassing love for God that propelled Spurgeon to great lengths in his ministry service, and this same kind of love can do the same for us as well.

## —An All-Consuming Love for the Word—

A natural extension of Spurgeon's love for the Lord was his love for God's Word. Spurgeon possessed a contagious enthusiasm for Scripture that overflowed into his messages, letters, and books. Spurgeon's love for the Bible manifest itself in at least three ways: He (1) held a high view of Scripture, (2) maintained a steady focus on Scripture, and (3) expressed complete dependence on God's Word.

### Spurgeon's High View of Scripture

Spurgeon treated the Bible as all that it claims to be: the authoritative, perfect, and effective Word of God Himself. His high view of Scripture communicated to his listeners that its message was trustworthy and that its promises would be fulfilled. A high view of the Bible, of course, results in a high view of God. One's view of God is only as high as one's view of Scripture. Those teachers who impress a low view of the Word upon their listeners will instill them with doubts about the reliability of Scripture and will cause them to arrive at erroneous conclusions about the Lord Himself. From his pulpit Spurgeon called the Bible "God's hand-writing,"[10] and at other times he said of the Scripture:

∞

*This volume is the writing of the living God: each letter was penned with an almighty finger, each word in it dropped from the everlasting lips, each sentence was dictated by the Holy Spirit . . . everywhere I find God speaking; it is God's voice, not man's; the words are God's words, the words of the Eternal, the Invisible, the Almighty, the Jehovah of the Earth.[11]*

*The Bible is a letter from Him, and we prize it beyond the finest gold.[12]*

*What the Spirit of God has written in this inspired Book is truth to us, and we allow no human teaching to rank side by side with it.[13]*

∞

The high view Spurgeon had of God's Word went hand in hand with his belief in the infallibility and inerrancy of Scripture:

∞

*It is also a book pure in the sense of truth, being without admixture of error. I do not hesitate to say that I believe there is no mistake whatever in the original holy scriptures from beginning to end . . . there is not an error of any sort in the whole compass of them.*[14]

*The Bible is a vein of pure gold, unalloyed by quartz, or any earthly substance. This is a star without speck; a sun without a blot; a light without darkness; a moon without its paleness; a glory without dimness. O Bible! It cannot be said of any other book, that it is perfect and pure; but of thee we can declare all wisdom is gathered up in thee, without a particle of folly. This is the judge that ends the strife, where wit and reason fail. This is the book untainted by any error; composed alone of pure, unalloyed, perfect truth.*[15]

∞

## Spurgeon's Steadfast Focus on Scripture

Every book Spurgeon wrote and every message he preached was thoroughly "bibline." Scripture was his starting point, his focus, and his guide for personal applications. A person cannot come away from any of Spurgeon's sermons without having learned one substantial truth or another from God's Word. Lewis Drummond tells us,

The Scriptures always played a central role in Spurgeon's life. Even as a small boy he knew the language of the Bible and many of the stories contained in the Scriptures. This was because of the good rootage he received in Stambourne from his grandfather James. . . . Immediately after his conversion he began to weigh every sermon in the light of the Word of God. . . . It was Spurgeon's deep conviction that the Bible imparts life, and that constitutes the essential secret of his spirituality.[16]

So deep were Spurgeon's convictions about the uniqueness and authority of God's Word that he told fellow ministers:

∞

*We have received the certainties of revealed truth. These are things which are verily believed among us. We do not bow down before men's theories of truth, nor do we admit that theology consists in "views" and "opinions." We declare that there are certain verities—essential, abiding, eternal—from which it is ruinous to swerve. I am deeply grieved to hear so many ministers talk as if the truth of God were a variable quantity, a matter of daily formation, a nose of wax to be constantly reshaped, a cloud driven by the wind. . . . Rest assured that there is nothing new in theology except that which is false; and that the facts of theology are today what they were eighteen hundred years ago.*[17]

*Nowadays, we hear men tear a single sentence of Scripture from its connection, and cry, "Eureka! Eureka!" as if they had found a new truth; and yet they have not discovered a diamond, but only a piece of broken glass. Had they been able to compare spiritual things with spiritual, had they understood the analogy of the faith, and had they been acquainted with the holy learning of the great Bible students of past ages, they would not have been quite so fast in vaunting their marvelous knowledge. Let us be thoroughly well acquainted with the great doctrines of the Word of God, and let us be mighty in expounding the Scriptures.*[18]

∞

Spurgeon's reverence for the Bible was such that he also had a healthy fear of inadvertently mishandling the Scriptures. He once said, "I would sooner a hundred times over appear to be inconsistent with myself than to be inconsistent with the Word of God."[19]

## Spurgeon's Complete Dependence on God's Word

Spurgeon said the Bible possesses the answer to every human need, and he communicated this truth in picturesque ways:

∞

*As I sat under a wide-spreading beech, I was pleased to mark with prying curiosity the singular habits of that most wonderful of trees, which seems to have an intelligence about it which other trees have not. I wondered and admired the beech, but I thought to myself, I do not think half as much of this beech as yonder squirrel does. I see him leap from bough to bough, and I feel sure that he dearly values the old beech tree, because he has his home somewhere inside it in a hollow place, these branches are his shelter, and those beechnuts are his food. He lives upon the tree. It is his world, his playground, his granary, his home; indeed, it is everything to him, and it is not so to me, for I find my rest and food elsewhere. With God's Word it is well for us to be like squirrels, living in it and living on it. Let us exercise our minds by leaping from bough to bough of it, and find our rest and food in it, and make it our all in all. There are hiding places in it; comfort and protection are there.[20]*

*As for us, we cast anchor in the haven of the Word of God. Here is our peace, our strength, our life, our motive, our hope, our happiness. God's Word is our ultimatum. Here we have it. Our understanding cries, "I have found it"; our conscience asserts that here is the truth; and our heart finds here a support to which all her affections can cling; and hence we rest content.[21]*

∞

## Spurgeon's Exhortations to Spiritual Leaders

In many of his lectures to fellow ministers, Spurgeon would inevitably remind them of the supreme place the Bible should have in their lives. He encouraged his peers toward a more passionate pursuit of God's Word as well as a more thorough dependence upon it. Here is just a sampling of the rich and thoughtful exhortations he proclaimed:

∞

### The Bible Is Inexhaustible

*After preaching the gospel for forty years, and after printing the sermons I have preached for more than six-and-thirty years, reaching now to the number of 2,200 in weekly succession, I am fairly entitled to speak about the fullness and richness of the Bible, as a preacher's book. Brethren, it is inexhaustible. No question about freshness will arise if we keep closely to the text of the sacred volume. There can be no difficulty as to finding themes totally distinct from those we have handled before; the variety is as infinite as the fullness. . . . In the forty years of my own ministry I have only touched the hem of the garment of divine truth; but what virtue has flowed out of it! The Word is like its Author, infinite, immeasurable, without end.*[22]

## The Bible Transforms Us

*The prayerful study of the Word is not only a means of instruction, but an act of devotion wherein the transforming power of grace is often exercised, changing us into the image of Him of whom the Word is a mirror.*[23]

## The Bible Is Our Strength and Success

*Men speak of waters that revive the spirits, and tonics that brace the constitution; but the Word of God has been more than this to us, times beyond count. Amidst temptations sharp and strong, and trials fierce and bitter, the Word of the Lord has preserved us. Amidst discouragements which damped our hopes, and disappointments which wounded our hearts, we have felt ourselves strong to do and bear, because the assurances of help which we find in our Bibles have brought us a secret, unconquerable energy.*[24]

## *The Bible Fills Us for Ministry Service*

*It was a very wet day the last time I was at Cologne, and I occupied a room in the hotel, which presented me with a highly picturesque view of a public pump. There was nothing else to see, and it rained so hard that I could not shift my quarters, so I sat and wrote letters, and glanced at the old pump. People came with pails for water, and one came with a barrel on his back, and filled it. In the course of an hour, that individual came several times; indeed, he came almost as often as all other comers put together, and always filled up his vessel. He was coming, and coming, and coming all the while; and I rightly concluded that he was a seller of water, and supplied other people; hence he came oftener than anybody else, and had a larger vessel. And that is precisely our condition. Having to carry the living water to others, we must go oftener to the well, and we must go with more capacious vessels than the general run of Christians. Look, then, to the vigor of your personal piety, and pray to be "filled with all the fullness of God."*[25]

∞

How often do we fill ourselves—our vessels—with the living water of God's Word so that we might freely dispense it to others? Are we filling ourselves abundantly so that we can give to others abundantly?

## —An All-Consuming Love That's Contagious—

No matter how long we've been Christians or how many times we've read the Bible, we can always grow in our love for God and His Word. There's always more to learn, more to appreciate, more to marvel over. And the more we fill ourselves with the infinite riches of our Lord and the Scriptures, the more those riches will naturally spill over the brim of our own lives into the lives of those around us. We can be like the seller of water who filled his pails at the public pump in Cologne and supplied other people with its life-giving nourishment. What a simple yet powerful way to have a positive impact on those under our leadership!

Also, because love is such a strong motivating force, it can help sustain us in the times when our work threatens to crush us . . . just as Spurgeon's love inspired him to persevere. We'll find ourselves looking upward at God rather than downward at our circumstances, and when we do so, we'll be able to see beyond that which is immediate and temporal and keep our focus on the eternal prize that awaits us.

# SPURGEON
## on His Knees

O LORD, we would cling to Thee more firmly than ever we have done. . . . We trust we can say also that we love the Lord, but Oh that we loved Him more! Let this blessed flame feed on the very marrow of our bones. May the zeal of Thine house consume us; may we feel that we love the Lord with all our heart, with all our mind, with all our soul, with all our strength, and hence may there be about our life a special consecration, an immovable dedication unto the Lord alone. . . .

O Lord Jesus, deepen in us our knowledge of Thee. . . . We would that the Word of God were more sweet to us, more intensely precious, that we had a deeper hunger and thirst after it. Oh that our knowledge of the truth were more clear and our grip of it more steadfast. Teach us, O Lord, to know the reason of the hope that is in us, and to be able to defend the faith against all comers. Plough deep in us, great Lord, and let the roots of Thy grace strike into the roots of our being, until it shall be no longer I that live, but "Christ that lives in me."[26]

# ᴬ Willingness
## *to* Suffer

"COUNT IT ALL JOY WHEN
YOU FALL INTO VARIOUS
TRIALS, KNOWING THAT THE
TESTING OF YOUR FAITH
PRODUCES PATIENCE."

—JAMES 1:2–3

In God's school of spiritual leadership, some courses are optional, but not Suffering 101. Rarely do we sign up for the course voluntarily; rather, the Schoolmaster Himself, in His perfect wisdom, will schedule us to take it when He knows we need it. That's only the beginning, of course, for there are many lessons for us to learn through suffering. And because they are frequently met with resistance on our part, we may find ourselves repeating the class. If we as leaders want to be truly useful in the Lord's work and refined as the finest gold—which has seen the greatest heat and the longest stay in the fires of the crucible—then we will submit willingly as the Lord walks with us not only through Suffering 101, but also Suffering 201, 301, 401, and beyond.

If we were to select a human professor for the course—one who is imminently qualified from personal experience— Charles Spurgeon would make an excellent choice. The twins Persecution and Affliction were lifelong occupants on the doorstep of his life, and their perpetual presence drove Spurgeon to recognize that the only solution was an utterly simple and complete dependence upon God alone. And the longer Spurgeon continued his work of ministry and exercised patience in the midst of suffering, the more He saw the Lord's consistent faithfulness in extracting spiritual gain and blessings from his difficult circumstances.

So that we can better understand and appreciate what Spurgeon taught about facing persecution and trials, let's first consider what he himself endured.

## —Spurgeon's Example in Suffering—

### His Response to External Attacks
When the New Park Street Chapel called Spurgeon to move to London and become their pastor, he was barely twenty years old. What's more, his style of preaching stood in marked

contrast to that of the other ministers of that day. Most ministers vied to outdo one another through elegant oratory and the presentation of clever poems and platitudes. Their sermons consisted of philosophy rather than Scripture. They sought approval in high societal circles, ignoring the city's working class and poor. Spurgeon, however, spoke in plain language and was direct. He taught the Scriptures not as an antiquated text, but a real and relevant guide. He spoke candidly about sin and people's need for a Savior. Almost overnight, New Park Street Chapel went from a virtually empty edifice to a congregation bursting at the seams. The common people, who were not getting their spiritual needs met elsewhere, came to Spurgeon in droves.

Spurgeon's youthfulness, forthright sermons, and immediate success were the ingredients that sparked the ire and suspicions of his peers and the press. Criticisms came from every direction and appeared in the newspapers frequently. Many predicted that Spurgeon was nothing more than a temporary sensation whose meteoric light would quickly burn out. And it's possible that would have indeed happened if Spurgeon had not already possessed a fierce resolve for serving God and an awareness that his duty was to the Lord and not men.

Still, the relentless onslaught weighed heavily on his heart. Susannah was distressed as well; and in *C. H. Spurgeon's Autobiography*, she revealed her thoughts on the matter and the action she took to encourage her husband:

My heart alternately sorrowed over him, and flamed with indignation against his detractors. For a long time, I wondered how I could set continual comfort before his eyes, till, at last, I hit upon the expedient of having the following verses printed in large Old English type, and enclosed in a pretty Oxford frame. . . .

> "Blessed are ye, when men shall revile you, and persecute you, and shall say all manner of evil against you falsely, for My sake. Rejoice, and be exceeding glad: for great is your reward in heaven: for so persecuted they the prophets which were before you." —Matthew v. 11, 12.

The text was hung up in our own room, and was read over by the dear preacher every morning—fulfilling its purpose most blessedly, for it strengthened his heart, and enabled him to buckle on the invisible armour, whereby he could calmly walk among men, unruffled by their calumnies, and concerned only for their best and highest interests.[1]

Evidently Spurgeon reached a point at which the opinions of others no longer mattered and his sole concern was to please God. He was able to say with the apostle Paul, "With me it is a very small thing that I should be judged by you or by a human court. . . . He who judges me is the Lord" (1 Corinthians 4:3–4). He said,

∞

*I am content to be criticized, misunderstood, and misrepresented. The cost was counted long ago, and the estimate was so liberal that there is no fear of its being exceeded. "I know whom I have believed, and am persuaded that He is able to keep that which I have committed unto Him against that day."²*

∞

On another occasion he stated,

∞

*Give me the comforts of God, and I can well bear the taunts of men. Let me lay my head on the bosom of Jesus, and I fear not the distraction of care and trouble. If my God will ever give me the light of his smile, and grant his benediction—it is enough. Come on foes, persecutors, fiends, ay, Apollyon himself, for "the Lord is my sun and shield." Gather, ye clouds, and environ me, I carry a sun within; blow, winds of the frozen north, I have a fire of living coal within; yea, death slay me, but I have another life— a life in the light of God's countenance.³*

∞

In fact, Spurgeon was able to recognize the good that could come out of people's negative intentions: "I am usually careless of the notices of papers concerning myself—referring all honours to my Master, and believing that dishonourable articles are but advertisements for me, and bring people under the sound of the Gospel."[4]

More significantly, Spurgeon didn't divide his energies between the Lord's work and defending himself. He preferred to stay wholly focused on his ministry and leave his detractors in the Lord's hands. But if the accusations became such that they necessitated a response, he was very competent at taking a stand and refuting or silencing his opposition. Biographer James Douglas noted, "Mr. Spurgeon had a great repugnance to the din of conflict. He was constitutionally pacific, and would sometimes prefer to sheath the sword rather than return the blow. At the same time, *unwillingness* is not to be confounded with *inability* to act the gladiator."[5]

Ultimately, Spurgeon arrived at the point where he could say,

∞

*I grew inured to falsehood and spite. The stings at last caused me no more pain than if I had been made of iron; but at first they were galling enough. Do not be surprised, dear friends, if you have the same experience; and if it comes, count it no strange thing, for in this way the saints have been treated in all time. Thank God, the wounds are not fatal, nor of long continuance! Time brings ease,*

*and use creates hardihood. No real harm has come
to any of us who have run the gauntlet of abuse; not
even a bruise remains.*[6]

∞

And in a sermon preached at Exeter Hall on June 15, 1856,
he advised,

∞

*Are you striving to do good, and do others impute
wrong motives to you? Do not be particular about
answering them; just go straight on, and your life
will be the best refutation of the calumny. . . . If any
man desires to reply to the false assertions of his
enemies, he need not say a word; let him go and do
good, that will be his answer.*[7]

∞

When it came to personal attacks, Spurgeon usually declined
to respond. However, if the matter involved God's church as
a whole, he would reluctantly enter the fray because of His
passion for protecting that which belonged to the Lord.

That was the case during the Down Grade Controversy, which
took place near the end of his life. Spurgeon recognized that
liberal theology was making inroads into the Baptist churches
of England, and through a series of articles in *The Sword and
the Trowel* he stated that this wayward thinking had put the

church on the "Down Grade." Tragically, Spurgeon found himself alone and at odds with many of his contemporaries, which devastated him. All through the controversy, Spurgeon endeavored to strike a careful balance between exhibiting a gracious spirit and maintaining an uncompromising stance. He focused solely on the issues at stake and not the personalities involved, as is evident in this excerpt from a lengthy letter he wrote to the ministers and delegates forming the Baptist Convention of the Maritime Provinces of Canada:

∞

*The pain I have felt in this conflict I would not wish any other man to share; but I would bear ten thousand times as much with eagerness if I could see the faith once for all delivered to the saints placed in honour among the Baptist churches of Great Britain. I resolved to avoid personalities from the very beginning; and, though sorely tempted to publish all that I know, I have held my peace as to individuals, and thus have weakened my own hands in the conflict. Yet this also I had rather bear than allow contention for the faith to degenerate into a complication of personal quarrels. I am no man's enemy, but I am the enemy of all teaching which is contrary to the Word of the Lord, and I will be in no fellowship with it.[8]*

∞

## His Response to Personal Afflictions

As if the sufferings from without weren't enough, Spurgeon also had to contend with afflictions from within, as we noted earlier. In one of the many letters he wrote while sick or bedridden, he described himself as "altogether stranded," noting, "I am not able to leave my bed, or to find much rest upon it. The pains of rheumatism, lumbago and sciatica, mingled together, are exceedingly sharp. I am aware I am dwelling in a body capable of the most acute suffering."[9]

Susannah had her own set of physical liabilities as well, and for much of their marriage was semi-invalid.

We cannot help but marvel at the fact that through all this and more, Spurgeon did not become bitter against God. Yes, he had his struggles; he had times when his faith was stretched seemingly to the limit, as noted by one biographer—but observe how he responded: "He had been through many a spell of doubt himself, and he once told the present writer that from time to time he was even tempted to question the existence of God. He generally met this temptation in his own case by recalling answers to prayer and cases of transformation of character by divine grace."[10]

In spite of his many difficult circumstances, Spurgeon trusted God and accepted his afflictions. When a critic told Spurgeon that his ills were due to the Lord's chastening, Spurgeon quipped, "I rejoice that I have such a God as that; and if He were to chasten me a thousand times worse than this, I would still love Him; yea, though He slay me, yet will I trust Him."[11]

## –Spurgeon's Instructions on Suffering–

### The Need for Suffering

Because Spurgeon was so well acquainted with persecution and trials, he had matured tremendously in this area of his spiritual life and had gained much wisdom that can help us, in turn, to persevere through whatever hardships we face. One key principle he desired for believers to recognize is that there are certain truths and promises in the Bible that have little or no meaning to us unless we have faced affliction:

∞

*Most of the grand truths of God have to be learned by trouble; they must be burned into us with the hot iron of affliction, otherwise we shall not truly receive them. No man is competent to judge in matters of the kingdom until first he has been tried; since there are many things to be learned in the depths which we can never know in the heights. We discover many secrets in the caverns of the ocean, which, though we had soared to heaven, we never could have known. He shall best meet the wants of God's people as a preacher who has had those wants himself; he shall best comfort God's Israel who has* needed comfort; and he shall best preach salvation who has felt his own need of it.[12]

I believe there is no place where we can learn so much, and have so much light cast upon Scripture, as we do in the furnace. Read a truth in tranquility, read it in peace, read it in prosperity, and you will not make anything of it. Be put inside the furnace (and nobody knows what a bright blaze is there who has not been there), and you will then be able to spell all hard words, and understand more than you could without it.[13]

The developing power of tribulation is very great: faith, patience, resignation, endurance, and steadfastness are by far the best seen when put to the test by adversity, pain, and temptation.[14]

Great hearts can only be made by great troubles. But more, the spade of trouble digs the reservoir of comfort deeper, and makes more room for consolation. God comes into our heart, He finds it full, He begins to break our comforts and to make it empty; then there is more room for grace. The humbler a man lies, the more comfort he will always have. . . . The more our troubles humble us, the more fit we *are to receive comfort: and God always gives us comfort when we are most fit for it.*[15]

∞

Suffering, then, makes us more complete in our spiritual growth and teaches us truths we would otherwise never learn.

## Our Companion in Suffering

The fact that we are guaranteed to encounter rough roads in life is not comforting. But there's another guarantee that should give us great comfort at all times: God will never make us walk these roads alone. He promises to be our constant companion—"I will never leave you nor forsake you" (Hebrews 13:5). There's no better companion we could ask for:

∞

*There is no riding to heaven in a chariot; the rough way must be trodden; mountains must be climbed, rivers must be forded, dragons must be fought, giants must be slain, difficulties must be overcome, and great trials must be borne. It is not a smooth road to heaven, believe me; for those who have gone but a very few steps therein have found it to be a rough one. It is a pleasant one; it is the most delightful in all the world; but it is not easy in itself, it is only pleasant because of the company, because of the sweet promises on which we lean, because of our*

Beloved who walks with us through all the rough
and thorny brakes of this vast wilderness.[16]

∞

## The Benefits of Suffering

In the same way that great heat and pressure can produce diamonds within beds of coal, persecution and trials can create
highly desirable qualities in our lives. Among several Spurgeon
mentioned are stronger faith and spiritual growth:

∞

*Perhaps the only way in which most men get their
faith increased is by great trouble. We do not grow
strong in faith on sunshiny days. It is only in rough
weather that a man gets faith. Faith is not an
attainment that droppeth like the gentle dew from
heaven; it generally comes in the whirlwind and the
storm. Look at the old oaks: how is it that they have
become so deeply rooted in the earth? Ask the
March winds and they will tell you. It was not the
April shower that did it, or the sweet May sunshine,
but it was March's rough wind.[17]*

*Storms and tempests are the things that make men
tough and hardy mariners. They see the works of
the Lord and His great wonders in the deep. So with
Christians. Great faith must have great trials.[18]*

*Until the oyster is sick it yields no pearls. Heavy damps of adversity make souls verdant. Saints, unlike the plants of earth, grow fastest in the sharpest weather. We make most progress in our voyage heavenward when the wind is rough: calms are more pleasant than profitable; better for comfort than for commerce; fairer in the present than in the retrospect. Affliction cuts the facets of the Lord's diamonds, and so they shine with a greater luster to His honor.*[19]

∾

Suffering can also bring about greater dependence on God:

∾

*Ah, it is well to be cast out of our depth, and made to swim in the sweet waters of mighty love! We know that it is supremely blessed to be compelled to cease from self, to surrender both wish and judgment, and to lie passive in the hands of God.*[20]

∾

Other benefits of suffering that Spurgeon noted are sympathy and greater compassion, as well as greater zeal and service:

∾

*If we have any power to console the weary, it is the result of our remembrance of what we once suffered—for here lies our power to sympathize.*[21]

*I would go into the deeps a hundred times to cheer a downcast spirit. It is good for me to have been afflicted, that I might know how to speak a word in season to one that is weary.*[22]

*The laborious pastor, the fervent minister, the ardent evangelist, the faithful teacher, the powerful intercessor, can all trace the birth of their zeal to the sufferings they endured through sin, and the knowledge they thereby attained of its evil nature. We have ever drawn the sharpest arrows from the quiver of our own experience. We find no swordblades so true in metal as those which have been forged in the furnace of soul-trouble.*[23]

∞

Suffering also leads to greater usefulness for ministry, Spurgeon noted.

∞

*I am sorry to say that I am made of such ill stuff that my Lord has to chasten me often and sorely. I am like a quill pen that will not write unless it be often nibbed, and therefore I have felt the sharp knife many times; and yet I shall not regret my pains and crosses so long as my Lord will write with*

*me on men's hearts. That is the cause of many min-
isters' afflictions; they are necessary to our work.*[24]

∽

## Our Response to Suffering

Affliction is always painful. Our initial reaction when we
encounter pain is to pull back, to avoid it. Yet when we consider that God can use our trials to shape us, develop us, and
touch the lives of others, we can see the wisdom of enduring
through our difficulties rather than circumventing them.

How can we respond positively to our suffering? How can we
encourage ourselves to keep moving forward? Spurgeon
offered several observations in that regard. First, we should
yield our concerns to God immediately. As we do so, we can
trust God to know our limits:

∽

*Cast your troubles where you have cast your sins;
you have cast your sins into the depth of the sea, there
cast your troubles also. Never keep a trouble half an
hour on your own mind before you tell it to your
heavenly Father. As soon as the trouble comes, quick,
the first thing, tell it to Him. Remember, that the
longer you delay telling your trouble to God, the more
your peace will be impaired. The longer the frost
lasts, the more likely that the ponds will be frozen.*[25]

*The knife of the heavenly Surgeon never cuts deeper than is absolutely necessary. A father smites no harder than duty constrains. "He doth not afflict willingly, nor grieve the children of men." A mother's heart cries, "Spare my child"; but no mother is more compassionate than our gracious God. When we consider how hard-mouthed we are, it is a wonder that we are not driven with a sharper bit. So much rust requires much of the file; but love is gentle of hand. The thought is full of consolation, that He who has fixed the bounds of our habitation, has also fixed the bounds of our tribulation.*[26]

∞

Next, Spurgeon acknowledged that sometimes we just won't understand God's reason for the pain or suffering. "Mysterious are the visitations of sickness," he once said, noting that when the Lord does "suspend [a person's] usefulness, it must be right, but the reason for it does not lie near the surface."[27] He later added,

∞

*Happily for us our happiness does not depend upon our understanding the providence of God: we are able to believe where we are not able to explain, and we are content to leave a thousand mysteries*

129

*unsolved rather than tolerate a single doubt as to*
*the wisdom and goodness of our heavenly Father.*[28]

∞

Concerning illness, Spurgeon reminded listeners of a paradoxical yet important truth: "Sickness has been frequently of more use to the saints of God than health has."[29]

Spurgeon pointed out two additional truths about our Lord that can keep us moving forward during suffering. Remember God can (1) turn bad into good, and (2) fill us—but only when we're empty.

∞

*Enemies have arisen, and they have been exceedingly violent, only to fulfil some special purpose of God, and increase our blessing against their will.*[30]

*God will have no strength used in His own battles but the strength which He Himself imparts . . . . Your emptiness is but the preparation for your being filled; and your casting down is but the making ready for your lifting up.*[31]

∞

## –The Bible's Encouragement to the Suffering–

Persevering through persecution or trials is never easy. As we endure the agony, we long for the cause of our affliction—whatever it might be—to go away. Sometimes the problem drags on and on, and we despair of ever getting out of it. We may begin to wonder if God has forgotten us, or resign ourselves to the possibility that our negative circumstances just aren't going to get any better. Then there are those afflictions that stay with us to the grave, such as a physical disability or a terminal illness.

Yet no matter how long or severe our suffering, we can take comfort in this: Every affliction is temporary. Our problems won't follow us to heaven. At most, they might continue through the rest of our lifetime, but even our lifespan is but an invisible speck of dust when placed on the timeline of eternity.

After the apostle Paul faced particularly harsh persecution, he said, "We do not lose heart. . . . For our light affliction, which is but for a moment, is working for us a far more exceeding and eternal weight of glory. . . . The things which are seen are temporary, but the things which are not seen are eternal" (2 Corinthians 4:16–18). Paul knew the future glory he experienced with the Lord in heaven would far outweigh the sufferings he faced on this earth. In the book of Romans, Paul said, "I consider that the sufferings of this present time are not worthy to be compared with the glory which shall be revealed in us" (8:18).

Most likely we will never look forward to suffering. We will always find it difficult to persevere through it. And many times, we won't understand the purpose of our afflictions. But there is one truth of which we can be absolutely certain: It's all temporary. It won't last long, comparatively speaking. By contrast, the joy and bliss that's ahead of us will last for all eternity. And that will be here before we know it.

# SPURGEON
## on His Knees

O LORD, we would humbly ask Thee to strengthen us as to our future confidence in Thee. Are there any of Thy servants here at this time, or anywhere all over the world, whose confidence begins to fail them by reason of present affliction or deep depression of spirit? We beseech Thee strengthen the things that remain that are ready to die, and let their faith no longer waver, but may they become strong in the Lord in full assurance of faith.

Oh God, Thou knowest the burden of every heart before Thee, the secret sighing of the prisoner cometh up into Thine ears. Some of us are in perplexity, others are in actual suffering of body. Some are sorely cast down in themselves, and others deeply afflicted with the trials of those they love, but as for all these burdens our soul would cast them on the Lord.

In quietness and confidence shall be our strength, and we . . . take up the place of sitting still, leaving with quiet acquiescence everything in the hands of God. Great Helmsman, Thou shalt steer the ship and we will not be troubled. By Thy grace we will leave everything most sweetly in Thy hands. Where else should these things be left? And we will take up the note of joyous song in anticipation of the deliverance which will surely come.[32]

# A Zeal *for* PROCLAIMING God's Word

"BE DILIGENT TO PRESENT YOUR-
SELF APPROVED TO GOD, A
WORKER WHO DOES NOT NEED
TO BE ASHAMED, RIGHTLY
DIVIDING THE WORD OF TRUTH."

—2 TIMOTHY 2:15

At the opening of the Metropolitan Tabernacle in March 1861, these were among Spurgeon's first words: "I would propose that the subject of the ministry of this house, as long as this platform shall stand, and as long as this house shall be frequented by worshipers, shall be the person of Jesus Christ."[1] And thirty years later, in what turned out to be his last sermon to his beloved people, he said,

∞

*If you wear the livery of Christ, you will find Him so meek and lowly at heart that you will find rest unto*

*your souls. He is the most magnanimous of captains. There never was His like among the choicest of princes. He is always to be found in the thickest part of the battle. When the wind blows cold He always takes the bleak side of the hill. The heaviest end of the cross lies ever on His shoulders. If He bids us carry a burden, He carries it also. If there is anything that is gracious, generous, kind, and tender, yea lavish and superabundant in love, you always find it in Him. His service is life, peace, joy. Oh, that you would enter on it at once![2]*

From the beginning of his ministry to the end, Spurgeon never wavered from his commitment to preach Christ and Him crucified and raised from the dead—he never failed to proclaim the fullness of the gospel message and the Word of God.

## –The Heart of Effective Preaching–

In relation to his preaching, Spurgeon said, "I take my text and make a bee-line to the cross." In a lecture at the Pastors' College, he stated,

∞

*Of all I would wish to say this is the sum; my brethren, preach CHRIST, always and evermore. He is the whole gospel. His person, offices, and work*

*must be our one great, all-comprehending theme. The world needs still to be told of its Savior, and of the way to reach Him. . . . We are not called to proclaim philosophy and metaphysics, but the simple gospel. Man's fall, his need of a new birth, forgiveness through an atonement, and salvation as the result of faith, these are our battle-ax and weapons of war.*[3]

∞

And on another occasion he said more succinctly: "Make Christ the diamond setting of every sermon."[4]

Some who heard Spurgeon's sermons accused him of narrowness, but Spurgeon's well-defined focus arose from his biblically based conviction that preachers and teachers are mouthpieces for God, and as such they need not garnish God's message and make it more enticing, but to proclaim it clearly and correctly.

∞

*Be it ours to give to the people what God gives to us. Be ye each of you as Micaiah, who declared, "As the Lord liveth, what the Lord saith unto me, that will I speak."*[5]

*It is not ours to improve the gospel, but to repeat it when we preach, and obey it when we hear.*[6]

*You need not bring life to the Scripture. You should draw life from the Scripture.*[7]

∞

What astonished many observers was that Spurgeon's direct style of preaching didn't drive people away; it did quite the opposite! Spurgeon stated well that a minister's foremost concern is not to make the Bible more appealing to people, but to let people know where they stood in relation to the Bible's truths:

∞

*Preach the doctrines of grace, dear brethren, and those who like not your Lord will either be changed themselves or change their minister. Preach the gospel very decidedly and firmly, no matter what people may say of you, and God will be with you. Some would like us to treat the Bible as if it were a peal of bells, sounding forth from a church steeple, which we can make to say whatever we please; rather let us sound forth Scriptural truth like a trumpet, giving a certain sound, that people may know that there is a meaning in it, and may learn at the same time what that meaning is.*[8]

∞

In an 1879 issue of *The Sword and the Trowel*, Spurgeon wrote,

∞

*The best attraction is the gospel in its purity. The weapon with which the Lord conquers men is the truth as it is in Jesus. The gospel will be found equal to every emergency: an arrow which can pierce the hardest heart, a balm which will heal the deadliest wound. Preach it, and preach nothing else. Rely implicitly upon the old, old gospel. You need no other nets when you fish for men; those your Master has given you are strong enough for the great fishes, and have meshes fine enough to hold the little ones. Spread these nets and no others, and you need not fear the fulfillment of His word, "I will make you fishers of men."[9]*

∞

And after more than twenty years of preaching to thousands every Sunday at the Metropolitan Tabernacle, the pastor said, "The best, surest, and most permanent way to fill a place of worship is to preach the gospel and to preach it in a natural, simple, interesting, earnest way."[10]

Spurgeon knew that Scripture had everything people truly needed, as affirmed by the psalmist:

The law of the Lord is perfect, converting the soul;
The testimony of the Lord is sure, making wise the simple;
The statutes of the Lord are right, rejoicing the heart;
The commandment of the Lord is pure, enlightening the eyes . . .

More to be desired are they than gold, yea, than much fine gold. (Psalm 19:7–8, 10)

Surely it was passages like this that inspired Spurgeon all the more to make statements such as these, which are excerpted from his famous lecture "The Greatest Fight in the World":

∞

*Sermons should be full of Bible; sweetened, strengthened, sanctified with Bible essence. The kind of sermons that people need to hear are outgrowths of Scripture. If they do not love to hear them, there is all the more reason why they should be preached to them. The gospel has the singular faculty of creating a taste for itself. Bible hearers, when they hear indeed, come to be Bible lovers.[11]*

*If we want weapons we must come here for them, and here only. Whether we seek the sword of offense or the shield of defense, we must find it within the volume of inspiration. If others have any other*

> storehouse, I confess at once I have none. I have
> nothing else to preach when I have got through with
> this book. Indeed, I can have no wish to preach at
> all if I may not continue to expound the subjects
> which I find in these pages. What else is worth
> preaching? Brethren, the truth of God is the only
> treasure for which we seek, and the Scripture is the
> only field in which we dig for it.[12]

This is not to say Spurgeon shunned other resources in his
sermon preparation. To the contrary, he was widely admired
for his knowledgeable grasp of many subjects. Lewis
Drummond points out that Spurgeon "was an avid reader of
the Puritans and a host of other authors as well."[13] Spurgeon
had a massive library numbering some twelve thousand volumes, and in addition to numerous Bible reference works and
commentaries, he had shelves filled with books on the sci-
ences, history, literature, and other subjects. Though he read
widely, he did so with one purpose, as one writer pointed out
shortly after the preacher's death:

> There never was a man more spontaneous in all he did,
> and less ambitious. He studied day and night, and
> filled his unerring memory with pious thoughts and
> suggestive histories, but it was never as men read for
> examinations, or even as men investigate for research

and discovery; it was solely with the object of winning souls to Christ. Whatever could be done for this end, with might and main he would do.[14]

Spurgeon also encouraged his Pastors' College students to draw sermon illustrations from the everyday world around them:

∞

*Watch for subjects as you go about the city or the country. Always keep your eyes and ears open, and you will hear and see angels. The world is full of sermons—catch them on the wing. A sculptor believes, whenever he sees a rough block of marble that there is a noble statue concealed within it, and that he has only to chip away the superfluities and reveal it. So do you believe that there is within the husk of everything the kernel of a sermon for the wise man.[15]*

∞

An anonymous biographer noted,

In the art of sermon illustration he stood unrivalled among his contemporaries. He was an omnivorous reader and a keen observer, and he cultivated the practice of turning everything to spiritual profit. The smallest incidents—such as the doings of his dog "Punch," the habits of birds, or the growth of the flowers—were constantly used to enforce divine truth.[16]

## –THE ESSENTIALS OF EFFECTIVE PREACHING–

Because preaching and teaching occupy such a significant part of a pastor's ministry, Spurgeon spoke frequently about them at the Pastors' College. A good portion of the messages that ended up in Spurgeon's three-volume set *Lectures to My Students* focused on preaching, with good reason: Many of the ministers of that day treated the Bible superficially in their messages, if at all. The deplorable state of church leadership in general was a catalyst that led to Spurgeon's decision to start the Pastors' College, where his main goal was to equip men to become qualified to preach and teach.

What are the hallmarks of an effective preacher or teacher? Spurgeon strongly urged his students and fellow ministers to (1) begin with prayer, (2) have a humble attitude, (3) invest time in preparation, (4) saturate themselves in the Word, (5) offer substance in the message, and (6) keep the message simple, interesting, and attractive.

### Begin with Prayer

As we saw earlier, all that Spurgeon did was bathed in prayer. He constantly lifted his thoughts, concerns, and needs to the Lord. Given that the works of preaching and teaching involve the communication of God's Word, it only makes sense that those who proclaim that Word ought to remain in constant communion with the One who brought it forth. He told his students, "Praying is the best studying."[17] He also told them, "A few minutes silent openness of soul before the Lord, has brought us more treasures of truth than hours of learned research."[18]

Spurgeon embraced the power of prayer and personal communion with God for the effective delivery of a message:

∞

*Prayer will singularly assist you in the delivery of your sermon; in fact, nothing can so gloriously fit you to preach as descending fresh from the mount of communion with God to speak with men. None are so able to plead with men as those who have been wrestling with God on their behalf.[19]*

*In order to have power in public, we must receive power in private. I trust that no brother here would venture to address his people without getting a message fresh from his Lord. If you deliver a stale story of your own concocting, or if you speak without a fresh anointing from the Holy One, your ministry will come to nothing. Words spoken on your own account, without reference to your Lord, will fall to the ground. When the footman goes to the door to answer a caller, he asks his master what he has to say, and he repeats what his master tells him. You and I are waiting-servants in the house of God, and we are to report what our God would have us speak. The Lord gives the soul-saving message, and clothes it with power; He gives it to a certain order of people, and under certain conditions.*[20]

∞

## Have a Humble Attitude

Among the challenges of speaking before an audience are resisting the temptations to seek the praise of our hearers and to credit ourselves for any success we might know. Our role, of course, is to point people to God, not ourselves. This is no light matter, and we would do well to take to heart these admonishments from Spurgeon:

∞

*I can say, and God is my witness, that I never yet feared the face of man, be he who or what he may; but I often tremble—yea, I always do—in ascending the pulpit, lest I should not faithfully proclaim the gospel to poor perishing sinners. The anxiety of rightly preparing and delivering a discourse, so that the preacher may fully preach Christ to his hearers, and pray them, in Christ's stead, to be reconciled to God, is such as only he knows who loves the souls of men. It is no child's play to be the occupant of a pulpit; he who finds it to be so may find it to be something more fearful than devil's play when the day of judgment shall come.*[21]

*It is a great mercy to be a minister. Preaching has often driven me to my knees and chained me to my Bible.*[22]

*If there be a place under high heaven more holy than another, it is the pulpit from which the gospel is preached. . . . When a man entereth, he may well put off his shoes from his feet, for the place whereon he standeth is holy.*[23]

∞

## Invest Time in Preparation

A minister who does not take the time to continually enrich himself spiritually will eventually become as a reservoir that has run dry. You cannot give out more than you take in. Thus preparation is an essential, or your people will become malnourished.

∞

*Your pulpit preparations are your first business, and if you neglect these, you will bring no credit upon yourself or your office. Bees are making honey from morning till night, and we should be always gathering stores for our people. I have no belief in that ministry which ignores laborious preparation.*[24]

*That which cost thought is likely to excite thought.*[25]

> *It is a waste of time, not an economy of it, to dispense with study, private prayer, and due preparation for your work.*[26]

∞

Spurgeon added that preparation needs to be coupled with a personal enthusiasm for the message. A sermon has to come not only from the mind, but the heart as well:

∞

> *So long as the life of the sermon is strengthened by preparation, you may prepare to the utmost; but if the soul evaporates in the process, what is the good of such injurious toil? It is a kind of murder which you have wrought upon the sermon which you have dried to death. . . . If there is fire, life, and truth in the sermon, then the quickening Spirit will work by it, but not else. Be earnest, and you need not be elegant.*[27]

∞

## Saturate Yourself in the Word

The effective preacher and teacher is well acquainted with Scripture. As Spurgeon put it, "I like to lie and soak in my text."[28] He also said,

∾

*In order to preach the gospel well, we must have such a knowledge of it that we are practically conversant with it. We must have it in our hearts. . . . Gather fresh manna every morning; gather it fresh from Heaven. Manna is all very well out of a brother's omer if I cannot go where it falls, but God's rule is for each man, to fill his own omer. Borrow from books if you will; but do not preach books, but the living Word. Get much inward knowledge, and then deal it out to your people.*[29]

∾

## Offer Substance in Your Message

Like a nourishing meal, a good sermon needs substance, Spurgeon argued:

∾

*Sermons should have real teaching in them, and their doctrine should be solid, substantial, and abundant. We do not enter the pulpit to talk for talk's sake; we have instructions to convey important to the last degree, and we cannot afford to utter pretty nothings.*[30]

*Put plenty into your sermons, gentlemen. After hearing some discourses I have been reminded of*

*the request of the farmer's boy to his missus when
eating his broth. "Missus, I wish you would let that
chicken run through this broth once more."*[31]

∞

## Keep Your Message Simple

Lewis Drummond wrote, "Spurgeon always said he was proud
of the fact that no one needed to bring a dictionary to the
Tabernacle whenever he preached."[32] And W. Y. Fullerton
stated: "Spurgeon introduced a new directness in preaching,
and he communicated it to his students. He taught them to
speak plainly and to articulate clearly."[33]

Spurgeon himself advocated clarity and simplicity:

∞

*Full many a time has a preacher rendered
Scripture dark by his explanations, instead of making it brighter. Many a preacher has been like a
painted window, shutting out the light instead of
admitting it.*[34]

*Christ said, "Feed My sheep. . . . Feed My lambs."
Some preachers, however, put the food so high that
neither lambs nor sheep can reach it. They seem to
have read the text, "Feed My giraffes."*[35]

∞

## Make the Message Interesting

Spurgeon wanted a compelling message. The extent to which Spurgeon disliked dull preaching is evident in the sarcasm he injected in this comment: "Dull preachers make good martyrs. They are so dry they burn well." [36] Of keeping it interesting, he also said:

∞

*Preach it [the gospel] in a natural, simple, interesting, earnest way.* [37]

*Christ Jesus was an attractive preacher; He sought above all means to set the pearl in a frame of gold, that it might attract the attention of the people. . . . It was no dull work to hear this King of preachers, He was too much in earnest to be dull, and too humane to be incomprehensible.* [38]

∞

## Make the Message Practical

Always aware of his listeners' needs, Spurgeon knew the importance of a practical message to address those needs. He once compared the choice of messages and content to preparing a well-conceived meal: "A wise householder labors to give to each one of the family his portion of meat in due season; he does not serve out rations indiscriminately, but suits the [meal] to the needs of the guests." [39]

Speaking of Charles Spurgeon's sermons, James Douglas observed that

> throughout the whole treatment, enforcement walks arm in arm with elucidation. The application is continuous. The hearer is under fire all the time. Each point has a practical bearing. . . . Another feature is the prominent place given to the Christ of history—"Jesus only" is the theme. The Written Word finds its main interpretation in the Incarnate Word.[40]

Spurgeon taught volumes about preaching and teaching, but if he had been asked to pare down his advice into one brief statement, he might have chosen this one, recorded by biographer William Williams:

∞

*Sermons fullest of Christ aimed directly at the heart, sermons that have been prayed over, and that are preached in connection with a praying people, these are sure to be blest.*[41]

∞

## –THE RESOURCES FOR EFFECTIVE PREACHING–

Spurgeon emphasized two resources for effective preaching: the Holy Spirit and the Bible. They remain powerful resources for preachers today.

## The Holy Spirit

Any attempt to teach God's Word to others is futile without the help of the Holy Spirit. As Spurgeon said,

∽

*To us, as ministers, the Holy Spirit is absolutely essential. Without Him our office is a mere name. . . . If we have not the Spirit which Jesus promised, we cannot perform the commission which Jesus gave.*[42]

∽

When Jesus explained to the disciples the role the Holy Spirit would have in their lives, He said, "When He, the Spirit of truth, has come, He will guide you into all truth" (John 16:13). That is, the Spirit is our instructor. Spurgeon echoed this when he said,

∽

*We have urgent need to study, for the teacher of others must himself be instructed. . . . If we are not instructed [by the Spirit], how can we instruct? . . . It is in our study-work, in that blessed labour when we are alone with the Book before us, that we need the help of the Holy Spirit. He holds the key of the heavenly treasury, and can enrich us beyond conception; He has the clue of the most labyrinthine doctrine, and can lead us in the way of truth.*[43]

∽

Spurgeon warned his students against going into the pulpit unprepared and assuming that the Holy Spirit would give them utterances, and he warned equally against preparation that was done without constant communion with and dependence upon God and the Spirit:

∞

*Habitually to come into the pulpit unprepared is unpardonable presumption: nothing can more effectively lower ourselves and our office.*[44]

*We ought to prepare the sermon as if all depended upon us, and then we are to trust the Spirit of God knowing that all depends upon Him.*[45]

*If there is to be a Divine result from God's Word, the Holy Ghost must go forth with it. As surely as God went before the children of Israel when He divided the Red Sea, as surely as He led them through the wilderness by the pillar of cloud and fire, so surely must the Lord's powerful presence go with His Word if there is to be any blessing from it. How, then, are we to get that priceless benediction? . . . Just as a certain form of electricity is produced by friction, so can we obtain power by coming in contact with God, and by means of the spiritual effect of truth as it operates upon a willing and obedient heart. To be*

*touched by the finger of God, yea, to come into
contact with even the hem of our Master's garment,
is to obtain heavenly energy; and if we have much of
it, we shall be charged with sacred strength in a
mysterious but very palpable way. Be much with
God in holy dialogue, letting Him speak to you by
His Word while you speak back to Him by your
prayers and praises. So far, you will obtain force.*[46]

∞

Not only does the Spirit instruct us, He also works through
our messages to bear results in the lives of our hearers. As
Spurgeon said, "We depend entirely upon the Spirit of God to
produce actual effect from the gospel."[47] He then added,

∞

*We do not stand up in our pulpits to display our
skill in spiritual sword play, but we come to actual
fighting: our object is to drive the sword of the Spirit
through men's hearts. . . . Aim at the right sort of
effect; the inspiring of saints to nobler things, the
leading of Christians closer to their Master, the
comforting of doubters till they rise out of their
terrors, the repentance of sinners, and their exercise
of immediate faith in Christ. Without these signs
following, what is the use of our sermons?*[48]

∞

With these effects in mind, Spurgeon concluded, "Our ends can never be gained if we miss the cooperation of the Spirit of the Lord. Therefore, with strong crying and tears, wait upon him from day to day."[49]

If we as leaders are not filled with the Spirit or walking in Him and thus are not dependent upon His empowerment, our deficiency will make itself evident as we attempt to fulfill our ministry obligations.

## The Bible

The other necessary resource for effective preaching is the Holy Scriptures.

Those whom God gifts to proclaim His Word are messengers, and the job description of a messenger is to transmit the contents of a message to its intended audience without impairing or embellishing it in any way. What's remarkable about the message entrusted to our care is its infinite breadth and depth. At times we may feel barren of ideas in our attempt to select a Bible text or topic for next week's sermon or lesson, but the fact is that Scripture presents us with an inexhaustible supply of truths we can communicate to our hearers.

∽

*I asked my grandfather, who had been in the ministry some fifty years, whether he was ever perplexed in choosing his theme. He told me frankly that this had always been his greatest trouble, compared with which, preaching in itself was no anxiety at all. I remember the venerable man's remark, "The difficulty is not because there are not enough texts, but because there are so many, that I am in a strait betwixt them." Brethren, we are sometimes like the lover of choice flowers, who finds himself surrounded by all the beauties of the garden, with permission to select but one. How long he lingers between the rose and the lily, and how great the difficulty to prefer one among ten thousand blooming lovelinesses!* [50]

*Our range of subjects is all but boundless, and we cannot, therefore, be excused if our discourses are threadbare and devoid of substance. If we speak as ambassadors for God, we need never complain of want of matter, for our message is full to overflowing.* [51]

∽

Indeed, Scripture gives us everything we need "for doctrine, for reproof, for correction, for instruction in righteousness, that the man of God may be complete, thoroughly equipped for every good work" (2 Timothy 3:16–17). So rich are its pages that we lack nothing in terms of what we can offer to our hearers. We need only to be sure that we are faithful to communicate its message clearly and accurately, and allow the Holy Spirit to do the rest.

## −A FINAL EXHORTATION REGARDING EFFECTIVE PREACHING−

We who are messengers of God's Word bear a serious responsibility—so much so that the apostle James said, "My brethren, let not many of you become teachers, knowing that we shall receive a stricter judgment" (3:1). Ours is a task, then, that deserves our best at all times. Spurgeon said as much in an 1883 issue of *The Sword and the Trowel*:

∞

*Sir Joshua Reynolds was one of the most distinguished painters of his day and, in answer to the inquiry, how he attained to such excellence, he replied, By observing, one simple rule, viz., to make each painting the best. Depend upon it that the same thing is true in the service of God. He who wishes to preach well should endeavor each time to preach his best. The audience may be small, and the hearers illiterate; but the best possible sermon will not be thrown away upon them.*[52]

∞

How are we doing? Are we doing our best? That's a question well worth asking from time to time, especially if we want the following words from Spurgeon to be true about ourselves:

∞

*Now, dear brethren, suffer one last word. You and I will ourselves soon die, unless our Master comes; and blessed will it be for us if, when we lie in the silent room, and the nights grow weary, and our strength ebbs out, we can stay ourselves upon the pillows, and say, "O Lord, I have known Thee from my youth, and hitherto have I declared Thy wondrous works; and now that I am about to depart, forsake me not." Thrice happy shall we be if we can say, in the last article, "I have not shunned to declare the whole counsel of God."*[53]

∞

# SPURGEON in the Pulpit

THE TRUE MINISTER of Christ knows that the true value of a sermon must lie, not in its fashion and manner, but in the truth which it contains. Nothing can compensate for the absence of teaching; all the rhetoric in the world is but as chaff to the wheat in contrast to the gospel of our salvation. However beautiful the sower's basket, it is a miserable mockery if it be without seed. The grandest discourse ever delivered is an ostentatious failure if the doctrine of the grace of God be absent from it; it sweeps over men's heads like a cloud, but it distributes no rain upon the thirsty earth; and therefore the remembrance of it to souls taught wisdom by an experience of pressing need is one of disappointment, or worse. . . .

Sound information upon scriptural subjects your hearers crave for, and must have. Accurate explanations of Holy Scripture they are entitled to, and if you are "an interpreter, one of a thousand," a real messenger of heaven, you will yield them plenteously.[54]

# CHAPTER EIGHT

# A Passion
## *for*
# Lost Souls

"WOE IS ME IF I DO NOT PREACH THE GOSPEL!"

—1 CORINTHIANS 9:16

As a leader, Spurgeon had many burdens weigh heavily on his heart, but none so heavily as the desire to see people come to salvation in Christ. His earnest passion was not only to preach about the Christ of the Bible, but also to urge his unconverted hearers to receive that same Christ into their hearts as their Savior. After all, Christ's own plea was for sinners to repent, and His purpose for coming to earth was to save the lost, so for Spurgeon to make evangelistic pleas to his listeners was merely to follow in the footsteps of the Master he loved so dearly.

Spurgeon's zeal for reaching out to the lost began early in his Christian life. Just a few short months after his conversion in 1850, he wrote to his mother, "I have seventy people whom I regularly visit on Saturday. I do not give a tract and go away; but I sit down and endeavour to draw their attention to spiritual realities."[1]

Especially touching was Spurgeon's genuine interest in the welfare of even just one soul. John B. Gough, a well-known temperance lecturer from America, was invited by Spurgeon to visit a very sick boy one day at the orphanage, and later, Gough shared,

> I had seen Mr. Spurgeon holding by his power sixty-five hundred people in breathless interest; I knew him as a great man universally esteemed and beloved; but as he sat by the bedside of a dying child, whom his beneficence had rescued, he was to me a greater and grander man than when swaying the mighty multitude at his will.[2]

Through all his years of ministry, Spurgeon's enthusiasm for leading people to Christ never waned. In his book *Around the Wicket Gate* he said, "We cannot too often or too plainly tell the seeking soul that his only hope for salvation lies in the Lord Jesus Christ."[3] Spurgeon echoed this refrain frequently in his lectures to his students and fellow ministers; in fact, the title of one such lecture says it all: "On Conversion as Our

Aim." This was indeed a key objective in Spurgeon's ministry, which is why the gospel message and the Bible's exhortations to sinners resonated clearly in all his sermons and writings.

Those who worked side by side with Spurgeon could not help but notice that the minister's greatest pleasure in serving the Lord came from seeing people receive Christ as their Savior. At a memorial service following Spurgeon's death, church elder J. T. Dunn commented,

> When persons came to enquire concerning salvation, or to confess their faith in the Lord Jesus Christ, how his eyes would brighten; and how heartily he would welcome them. It mattered not to him what the character of the clothing, or what the age of the candidate. He could always meet their condition, and tenderly sympathize with them. Many a one have I seen go into that vestry with a tearful eye, who has returned with joy on the countenance.[4]

Friend W. Y. Fullerton believed it was this very passion that had much to do with Spurgeon's popularity:

> I confess that when I had the privilege of a little talk with Mr. Spurgeon I have looked at him, and listened to him, and said to myself, "What is there in this man that has made him the most popular preacher that ever spoke the English tongue?" I have always believed that the chief secret of his attractiveness was the fact that, in

every sermon, no matter what the text or the occasion, he explained the way of salvation in simple terms. There are thousands of people everywhere who, beneath their superficial indifference or apparent opposition, long in their hearts to know what they must do to be saved.[5]

## –A HEART FOR REACHING THE LOST–

It has been said that Jesus' last command should be our first concern: "Go therefore and make disciples of all the nations" (Matthew 28:19). Our tendency is to view Christ's words as a mandate to send workers into the mission field, but for every Christian, the mission field is his or her immediate vicinity. Some object that our Lord's command applied only to the disciples, but the sweeping scope of His commission and His promise to be with us "to the end of the age" (verse 20) speaks of a work that is carried on through successive generations of Christians.

The apostle Paul, in the closing words of his second letter to Timothy, summarized Timothy's responsibilities as a church leader, exhorting him to "do the work of an evangelist" (2 Timothy 4:5). Paul was not calling his protégé to the office of an evangelist, but to do the work itself—to make soul-winning a part of his ministry. Undoubtedly, Paul's motive was a love for the lost—a love modeled by Jesus Christ Himself.

Fullerton says of Spurgeon, "It was this love for the souls of men that he sought by word and example to instill into his disciples."[6] Among Spurgeon's exhortations to other leaders—exhortations that hearken to us today—are these:

∽

*Soul-winning is the chief business of the Christian minister, indeed, it should be the main pursuit of every true believer.*[7]

*Do you ever mourn over your hearers as one that weepeth for the slain of his people? Can you bear that they should pass away to judgment unforgiven? Can you endure the thought of their destruction? I do not know how a preacher can be much blessed of God who does not feel an agony when he fears that some of his hearers will pass into the next world impenitent and unbelieving.*[8]

*We must capture hearts for Jesus by showing that we are of like passions with them, and love them much. Love men to Jesus—that is the art of soul-winning.*[9]

*Go on to win other souls. It is the only thing worth living for. God is much glorified by conversions, and therefore this should be the great object of life.*[10]

*You do not love the Lord at all unless you love the souls of others.*[11]

∽

In a lecture to a large group of ministers, Spurgeon spoke on five essentials every leader ought to pursue in perfecting his ministry. One of those essentials was love: "Assuredly we must abound in love."[12] He went on to say that along with an intense love for God and our work,

∞

*We must have also intense love to the souls of men, if you are to influence them for good. Nothing can compensate for the absence of this. Soul-winning must be your passion, you must be born to it; it must be the very breath of your nostrils, the only thing for which you count life worth the having.*[13]

∞

We're to extend this love even to those who despise us, in the spirit of Christ's command in Matthew 5:44 to love our enemies:

∞

*We ought to have an intense longing for the salvation of all sorts of men, and especially for those, if there are any, that treat us badly. We should never wish them ill, not for a moment; but in proportion to their malice should be our intense desire for their good.*[14]

∞

And in case any minister might object that he has neither the gift nor the training to evangelize, Spurgeon also said,

∞

*I hope it will never get to be your notion that only a certain class of preachers can be soul-winners. Every preacher should labor to be the means of saving his hearers. The truest reward of our life work is to bring dead souls to life. I long to see souls brought to Jesus every time I preach. It should break my heart if I did not see it to be so. Men are passing into eternity so rapidly that we must have them saved at once. . . . If our preaching never saves a soul, and is not likely to do so, should we not better glorify God as peasants, or as tradesmen? What honor can the Lord receive from useless ministers? . . . Brethren, can we bear to be useless? Can we be barren, and yet content?*[15]

∞

## –THE PREREQUISITES FOR REACHING THE LOST–

### Reliance upon God

Spurgeon was one who cried out to God over the souls of men before he cried out to men about God. He said that "winners of souls must first be weepers for souls,"[16] recognizing that without the Lord's empowerment, any effort on our part is empty and futile.

∞

*As for you and for me, what can we do in saving a soul from death? Of ourselves nothing, any more than that pen which lies upon the table could write the Pilgrim's Progress; yet let a Bunyan grasp the pen, and the matchless work is written. So you and I can do nothing to convert souls till God's eternal Spirit takes us in hand but then He can do wonders by us, and get to Himself glory by us, while it shall be joy enough to us to know that Jesus is honoured, and the Spirit magnified. . . . This is golden wages for a man who really loves his Master; Jesus is glorified, sinners are saved.*[17]

∞

## An Emptying of Oneself

Our reliance upon God, of course, requires a corresponding emptying of self and a proper fear of the responsibility we bear in proclaiming the gospel rightly and faithfully:

∞

*I have preached the gospel now these thirty years and more, and some of you will scarcely believe it, but before I come to address the congregation in this Tabernacle, I tremble like an aspen leaf. And often, in coming down to this pulpit, have I felt my knees knock*

*together—not that I am afraid of any one of my hear-*
*ers, but I am thinking of that account which I must*
*render to God, whether I speak His Word faithfully or*
*not. On this service may hang the eternal destinies of*
*many. O God, grant that we may all realize that this*
*is a matter of the most solemn concern.*[18]

∞

## –THE WORK OF REACHING THE LOST–

Given that we, as God's ambassadors, have the privilege of expressing His compassion to the unsaved, let's consider Spurgeon's advice on how we can best equip ourselves for the work of winning souls.

### A Heart Filled with Empathy

We are most powerfully able to minister to another person when we ourselves have experienced the same trial or circumstance faced by that person. If we've walked in that person's shoes, then we know what kind of guidance will help most—all because we've "been there."

Likewise, we are best able to love and empathize with sinners when we recall the former state from which Christ rescued us:

∞

*Brethren, we shall never preach the Savior of sin-*
*ners better than when we feel ourselves to be the*

169

*sinners whom He came to save. A penitent mourning for sin [prepares] us to preach repentance. "I preached," says John Bunyan, "sometimes, as a man in chains to men in chains, hearing the clanking of my own fetters while I preached to those who were bound in affliction and iron." Sermons wrung out of broken hearts are often the means of consolation to despairing souls. It is well to go to the pulpit, at times, with "God be merciful to me a sinner" as our uppermost prayer.*[19]

*A great heart is the main qualification for a great soul-winner.*[20]

∞

## A Plea That Loves and Warns

When it comes to sharing the gospel message, a widespread problem among Christians (including church leaders) is the hesitancy to explain to unbelievers that the punishment for an unrepentant heart is eternal condemnation. Because we want to make Christ look as attractive as possible, we usually say little in the way of warnings. While it is true that a positive encouragement usually draws more people than a negative exhortation, we must keep in mind that our failure to mention the future punishment of sinners puts an unbeliever in the position of making a decision based on ignorance. We do no favors by such neglect. So, while it's difficult to warn sinners of the consequences of staying in their sin, still, it's essential. The key is to proclaim our warnings within the larger context of Christ's love. Spurgeon offered some wise words on this matter:

∽

*The vital truth of our Lord's expiation must be preached often, clearly, and with emphasis; and, if it be not so, we have not correctly learned Christ, neither shall we successfully teach Him. To attempt to preach Christ without His cross, is to betray Him with a kiss.[21]*

*Sometimes, right solemnly, the sacred mysteries of eternal wrath must be preached, but far oftener let us preach the wondrous love of God. There are more souls won by wooing than by threatening. It is not hell, but Christ, we desire to preach. O sinners! We are not afraid to tell you of your doom, but we do not choose to be for ever dwelling on that doleful theme. We rather love to tell you of Christ, and Him crucified. We want to have our preaching rather full of the frankincense of the merits of Christ, than of the smoke and fire, and terrors of Mount Sinai; we are not come unto Mount Sinai, but unto Mount Zion—where milder words declare the will of God, and rivers of salvation are abundantly flowing.[22]*

*We shall never persuade men if we are afraid to speak of the judgment and the condemnation of the unrighteous. None [is] so infinitely gracious as our Lord Jesus Christ, yet no preacher ever uttered more faithful words of thunder than He did. It was He who spoke of the place "where their worm dieth not and their fire is not quenched." It was He who said, "These shall go away into everlasting punishment." It was He who spake the parable concerning that man in hell who longed for a drop of water to cool his tongue. We must be as plain as Christ was, as downright in honesty to the souls of men, or we may be called to account for our treachery at the last. If we flatter our fellows into fond dreams as to the littleness of future punishment, they will eternally detest us for so deluding them, and in the world of woe they will invoke perpetual curses upon us for having prophesied smooth things, and having withheld from them the awful truth.*[23]

∞

## A Zeal for One as Well as Many

When it comes to ministry, it's not the number of people under your influence that counts, but the quality of your influence. Speaking of Andrew's diligence in bringing Peter to Jesus, Spurgeon said,

∞

*Andrew proved his wisdom in that he set great store by a single soul. He bent all his efforts at first upon one man. Afterwards, Andrew, through the Holy Spirit, was made useful to scores, but he began with one. What a task for the arithmetician, to value one soul! One soul sets all heaven's bells ringing by its repentance. One sinner that repenteth maketh the angels rejoice. What if you spend a whole life pleading and labouring for the conversion of that one child? If you win that pearl it shall pay you your life worth. Be not therefore dull and discouraged because your class declines in numbers, or because the mass of those with whom you labour reject your testimony. . . . Be content, and labour in your sphere, even if it be small, and you will be wise.*[24]

*Remember, dear brother, if you give your whole soul to the charge committed to you, it does not matter much about its appearing to be a somewhat small and insignificant affair, for as much skill may be displayed in the manufacture of a very tiny watch as in the construction of the town clock; in fact, a minute article may become the object of greater wonder than another of larger dimensions. Quality is a far more precious thing than quantity.*[25]

∞

No matter how limited our sphere, then, let us serve with diligence.

## A Belief That God's Word Will Bear Results

Spurgeon entered the pulpit literally expecting that unconverted hearers would respond to the gospel message. He also placed his full trust in God's ability to convict a person as opposed to his own ability to persuade:

∞

*B*eloved, have a genuine faith in the Word of God, and in its power to save. *Do not go up into the pulpit preaching the truth, and saying, "I hope some good will come of it" but confidently believe that it will not return void, but must work the eternal purpose of God. Do not speak as if the gospel might have some power, or might have none.*[26]

∞

## A LEGACY OF REACHING THE LOST

W. Y. Fullerton tells us that Spurgeon, in a sermon spoken during the earlier years of his ministry, imagined a scene at his own funeral and expressed this desire concerning it:

∞

*A*nd when you see my coffin carried to the silent grave, I should like every one of you, whether converted or not, to be constrained to say, "He did *earnestly urge us, in plain and simple language, not to put off the consideration of eternal things; he did entreat us to look to Christ. Now he is gone, our blood is not at his door if we perish."*[27]

∞

At the end of his years, Spurgeon could say he had not failed to preach the way of salvation in any of his thousands of sermons. As a fisher of men, he cast the net far and wide, always seeking new prospects, always trusting God to bear the fruit. He cast the net differently each time so as to avoid repetition or monotony. He kept his plea relevant to the text on which he was preaching, being careful not to abuse Scripture in the course of presenting the gospel. And the wellspring of it all was a tender heart that earnestly wept for sinners to be reconciled to God.

Upon his deathbed, Spurgeon insisted that only the letters "C. H. S." be inscribed upon his tomb. But given his legacy, those nearest to him could not help but add two verses from Spurgeon's favorite hymn—verses that describe succinctly a major focus and passion of his forty years in ministry:

> E'er since by faith I saw the stream
> > Thy flowing wounds supply,
> Redeeming love has been my theme,
> > And shall be till I die;

Then in a nobler, sweeter song,
     I'll sing Thy power to save,
When this poor lisping, stammering tongue
     Lies silent in the grave.[28]

# SPURGEON with His Pen

IN THAT DAY when I surrendered myself to my Saviour, I gave Him my body, my soul, my spirit; I gave Him all I had, and all I shall have for time and for eternity. I gave Him all my talents, my powers, my faculties, my eyes, my ears, my limbs, my emotions, my judgment, my whole manhood, and all that could come of it, whatever fresh capacity or new capability I might be endowed with.[29]

*—From C. H. Spurgeon's autobiography, in reflection upon the day of his salvation*

I vow to glory alone in Jesus and His cross, and to spend my life in the extension of His cause, in whatsoever way He pleases. I desire to be sincere in this solemn profession, having but one object in view, and that to glorify God. Blessing upon Thy name that Thou hast supported me through the day; it is Thy strength alone that could do this. . . . Thou hast enabled me to profess Thee, help me now to honour Thee, and carry out my profession, and live the life of Christ on earth![30]

*—Written by Spurgeon in his diary on the day of his baptism, May 3, 1850*

# THE POWER OF A SINGLE FOCUS

∞

All through this book, we have looked to C. H. Spurgeon's example as a source of inspiration and encouragement in our own growth toward greater spiritual leadership. And we're going to do that again one last time.

It's obvious from the phenomenal results of Spurgeon's ministry that God used him in mighty ways. Of course, everything Spurgeon accomplished was made possible by God Himself and the power of the Holy Spirit. Take these divine resources out of the equation, and Spurgeon would have amounted to nothing. No amount of human effort can even begin to match divine enablement.

Spurgeon knew that—and that's part of what made him such an outstanding spiritual leader. His credo was, "Not I, but

Christ." He knew that the greatest power of all came from above. His total reliance upon divine enablement made him a more mighty instrument in the hands of God.

Yet Spurgeon also knew that the more he concentrated his energies toward a single goal—that of pleasing and glorifying God—the more God could do through him. When we scatter our energies and attention in several different directions, it's difficult for us to have a very significant impact on any one area of our lives. It's only when we elect to do a few things well that we are able to do each of those things better. Can you imagine, then, the effect we would have if all our energies were poured into just one goal?

The power of having a single focus is well illustrated by a beam of light. Normally, light rays are cast in all directions, which diffuses their impact. But the more you focus a beam of light, the more powerful it becomes—to the point that a highly focused laser beam is strong enough to cut through steel.

As you read about each of Spurgeon's leadership qualities, did you notice the underlying theme running through every quality and every task was a single focus upon glorifying God? While it's true he divided his energies across several ministry endeavors, his every effort merged toward a single goal.

Read the following quotes slowly. Don't rush through them. Ponder what your life, your leadership, your ministry service would look like if these statements were true about you:

∞

*G*od deserves to be served with all the energy of which we are capable.[1]

*I* know of nothing which I would choose to have as the subject of my ambition for life than to be kept faithful to my God till death.[2]

*W*e must see to it that His glory is the one sole object of all we do.[3]

*W*hether we are servants or masters, whether we are poor or rich, let us take this as our watchword, "As to the Lord, and not to men." Henceforth may this be the engraving of our seal and the motto of our coat-of-arms; the constant rule of our life and the sum of our motive.[4]

*K*eep not back part of the price. Make a full surrender of every motion of thy heart; labour to have but one object, and one aim. And for this purpose give God the keeping of thine heart. Cry out for more of the divine influences of the Holy Spirit, that so when thy soul is preserved and protected by Him, it may be directed into one channel, and one only, that thy life may run deep and pure, and clear and peaceful;

its only banks being God's will, its only channel the love of Christ and a desire to please Him.[5]

You are the branded servants of Christ, bearing in your bodies His mark. You have now no liberty to serve another, you are the sworn soldiers of the Crucified.[6]

Excel also in one power, which is both mental and moral, namely, the power of concentrating all your forces upon the work to which you are called. Collect your thoughts, rally all your faculties, mass your energies, focus your capacities. Turn all the springs of your soul into one channel, causing it to flow onward in an undivided stream. Some men lack this quality. They scatter themselves, and therefore fail. Mass your battalions, and hurl them upon the enemy. Do not try to be great at this, and great at that—to be "everything by starts, and nothing long"; but suffer your entire nature to be led in captivity by Jesus Christ, and lay everything at His dear feet who bled and died for you.[7]

"Jesus only" must be the motive and motto of your life-course. It is the duty of a steward to be devoted to the interests of his master; and if he forgets this *for any other object, however laudable that object may be, he is not faithful. We cannot afford to let our lives run in two channels; we have not enough life-force for two objects. We need to be whole-hearted. We must learn to say, "One thing; I do."* [8]

*I pray God, if I have a drop of blood in my body which is not His, to let it bleed away; and if there be one hair in my head which is not consecrated to Him, I would have it plucked out.* [9]

∞

Though the words are different, ultimately, the focal point is always the same: Not I, but Christ. And this doesn't apply only to our spiritual service, it applies to everything we do. As the apostle Paul said in 1 Corinthians 10:31, "Whether you eat or drink, or whatever you do, do *all* to the glory of God" (italics added). We're called to total surrender as a living sacrifice that stays upon the altar of service to God, holding nothing back. It helps, too, when we carefully choose to do only a few things well rather than many—a few things that can readily and ultimately merge into the single focus of glorifying God.

Do you long to be more useful to God? To let Him do what He *really* wants to do through you? To let Him "do exceedingly abundantly above all that we ask or think, according to the power that works in us" (Ephesians 3:20)?

Not I, but Christ.

Is that your heart's desire?

If so, God can—and will—use you.

**CHAPTER ONE—A PASSION FOR PRAYER**

1. W. Y. Fullerton, *Charles Haddon Spurgeon* (Chicago: Moody, 1966), 150.

2. *C. H. Spurgeon's Prayers* (London: Passmore & Alabaster, 1905), vi.

3. Fullerton, *Charles Haddon Spurgeon*, 149.

4. C. H. Spurgeon, *The Metropolitan Tabernacle Pulpit*, vol. 49 (London: Passmore & Alabaster, 1903), 476.

5. C. H. Spurgeon, "The Importunate Widow," *The Metropolitan Tabernacle Pulpit*, vol. 15 (1869), from The C. H. Spurgeon Collection, version 2.0 (Rio, Wisc.: AGES Software, 2001).

6. C. H. Spurgeon, *Lectures to My Students*, vol. 1 (Grand Rapids: Baker Book House, 1987), 49.

7. C. H. Spurgeon, *Able to the Uttermost*, chapter 15 from The C. H. Spurgeon Collection, version 2.0 (Rio, Wisc.: AGES Software, 2001).

8. Spurgeon, "True Prayer—True Power!" *The Metropolitan Tabernacle Pulpit*, vol. 6 (1860), from The C. H. Spurgeon Collection.

9. Spurgeon, *The Metropolitan Tabernacle Pulpit*, vol. 1 (London: Passmore & Alabaster, 1855), 122.

10. C. H. Spurgeon, *An All-Round Ministry* (Carlisle, Pa.: The Banner of Truth Trust, 1978), 313.

11. Fullerton, *Charles Haddon Spurgeon*, 46.

12. Spurgeon, "A New Order of Priests and Levites," *The Metropolitan Tabernacle Pulpit*, vol. 17 (1871), from The C. H. Spurgeon Collection.

13. Spurgeon, *Lectures to My Students*, vol. 1: 47.

14. Spurgeon, *An All-Round Ministry*, 314.

15. Ibid., 13.

16. C. H. Spurgeon, *The Check Book of the Bank of Faith* (Fort Washington, Pa.: Christian Literature Crusade, 1960), 31.

17. Spurgeon, "Order and Argument in Prayer," *The Metropolitan Tabernacle Pulpit*, vol. 12 (1866), from The C. H. Spurgeon Collection.

18. Spurgeon, *Lectures to My Students*, vol. 1: 41.

19. Ibid., 62.

20. Ibid., 49.

21. Spurgeon, "Carried by Four," *The Metropolitan Tabernacle Pulpit*, vol. 17 (1871), from The C. H. Spurgeon Collection.

22. Spurgeon, "All at It," *The Metropolitan Tabernacle Pulpit*, vol. 34 (1888), from The C. H. Spurgeon Collection.

23. Spurgeon, *An All-Round Ministry*, 220.

24. Spurgeon, *Lectures to My Students*, vol. 1: 55–56.

25. Spurgeon, "The Chariots of Amminadab," *The Metropolitan Tabernacle Pulpit*, vol. 20 (1874), from The C. H. Spurgeon Collection.

26. Spurgeon, "The Throne of Grace," *The Metropolitan Tabernacle Pulpit*, vol. 17 (1871), from The C. H. Spurgeon Collection.

27. Spurgeon, "Pray Without Ceasing," *The Metropolitan Tabernacle Pulpit*, vol. 18 (1872), from The C. H. Spurgeon Collection.

28. Spurgeon, *The Metropolitan Tabernacle Pulpit*, vol. 24 (London: Passmore & Alabaster, 1878), 258.

29. Spurgeon, "Pray Without Ceasing," *The Metropolitan Tabernacle Pulpit*, vol. 18 (1872), from The C. H. Spurgeon Collection.

30. C. H. Spurgeon, "Special Protracted Prayer," *The Metropolitan Tabernacle Pulpit*, vol. 14 (1868), from The C. H. Spurgeon Collection.

31. Spurgeon, "The Holy Spirit's Intercession," *The Metropolitan Tabernacle Pulpit*, vol. 26 (1880), from The C. H. Spurgeon Collection.

32. Spurgeon, "An Assuredly Good Thing," *The Metropolitan Tabernacle Pulpit*, vol. 15 (1869), from The C. H. Spurgeon Collection.

33. Terry W. Glaspey, *Pathways to the Heart of God* (Eugene, Ore.: Harvest House, 1998), 95.

34. Spurgeon, "Prayer Answered, Love Nourished," *The Metropolitan Tabernacle Pulpit*, vol. 5 (1859), from The C. H. Spurgeon Collection.

35. Ibid.

36. Ibid.

37. *C. H. Spurgeon's Prayers*, 148.

38. Spurgeon, *Able to the Uttermost*, chapter 15 from The C. H. Spurgeon Collection, version 2.0 (Rio, Wisc.: AGES Software, 2001).

39. Spurgeon, "A Psalm for the New Year," *The Metropolitan Tabernacle Pulpit*, vol. 8 (1862), from The C. H. Spurgeon Collection.

40. Spurgeon, *The Metropolitan Tabernacle Pulpit*, vol. 19 (London: Passmore & Alabaster, 1873), 218.

41. Spurgeon, "The Minister's Plea," *The Metropolitan Tabernacle Pulpit*, vol. 19 (1873), from The C. H. Spurgeon Collection.

42. Spurgeon, "Daniel: A Pattern for Pleaders," *The Metropolitan Tabernacle Pulpit*, vol. 61 (1915), from The C. H. Spurgeon Collection.

43. Spurgeon, *The Metropolitan Tabernacle Pulpit*, vol. 41 (London: Passmore & Alabaster, 1895), 518.

44. *C. H. Spurgeon's Prayers*, 2–4.

**Chapter 2—A Faith That Endures**

1. Eric W. Hayden, *Highlights in the Life of Charles Haddon Spurgeon*, chapter 52 from The C. H. Spurgeon Collection, version 2.0 (Rio, Wisc.: AGES Software, 2001).

2. Ibid.

3. Spurgeon, *The Metropolitan Tabernacle Pulpit*, vol. 21 (London: Passmore & Alabaster, 1875), 149.

4. John Blanchard, ed., *Gathered Gold* (London: Evangelical Press, 1984), 92.

5. Edmond Hez Swem, ed., *Spurgeon's Gold* (New York: Robert Carter & Brothers, 1888), 56.

6. Spurgeon, *The Metropolitan Tabernacle Pulpit*, vol. 3 (London: Passmore & Alabaster, 1857), 3.

7. C. H. Spurgeon, *The Check Book of the Bank of Faith* (Fort Washington, Pa.: Christian Literature Crusade, 1960), vi.

8. Ibid., vii.

9. C. H. Spurgeon, *An All-Round Ministry* (Carlisle, Pa.: The Banner of Truth Trust, 1978), 185.

10. Spurgeon, *The Metropolitan Tabernacle Pulpit*, vol. 41 (London: Passmore & Alabaster, 1895), 101.

11. Spurgeon, *An All-Round Ministry*, 183.

12. Ibid., 183.

13. Ibid., 3–4.

14. Ibid., 202.

15. Ibid., 19–21.

16. Ibid., 22–23.

17. Ibid., 16.

18. C. H. Spurgeon, *Gleanings Among the Sheaves* from The C. H. Spurgeon Collection, version 2.0 (Rio, Wisc.: AGES Software, 2001).

19. Archives, Spurgeon's College, London, as cited in Lewis Drummond, *Spurgeon: Prince of Preachers* (Grand Rapids: Kregel, 1992), 456.

20. Spurgeon, "Mature Faith—Illustrated by Abraham's Offering Up Isaac," *The Metropolitan Tabernacle Pulpit*, vol. 15 (1869), from The C. H. Spurgeon Collection.

21. Spurgeon, "A Lecture for Little-Faith," *The Metropolitan Tabernacle Pulpit*, vol. 4 (1858), from The C. H. Spurgeon Collection.

22. C. H. Spurgeon, "Sermons to Ministers and Other Tried Believers," *Unusual Occasions* from The C. H. Spurgeon Collection, version 2.0 (Rio, Wisc.: AGES Software, 2001).

23. Swem, ed., *Spurgeon's Gold*, 75.

24. Spurgeon, *An All-Round Ministry*, 279.

25. Ibid., 281.

26. Ibid., 366.

## Chapter 3—A Commitment to Holiness

1. W. Williams, *Personal Reminiscences of Charles Haddon Spurgeon* (London: The Religious Tract Society, 1895), 13.

2. C. H. Spurgeon, *Spurgeon's Gems* (London: Passmore & Alabaster, 1859), 280.

3. C. H. Spurgeon, *Lectures to My Students*, vol. 1 (Grand Rapids: Baker, 1987), 2–3.

4. Susannah Spurgeon and J. W. Harrald, *C. H. Spurgeon's Autobiography*, vol. 3 (London: Passmore & Alabaster, 1899), 159.

5. Spurgeon, *Lectures to My Students*, vol. 1: 12.

6. C. H. Spurgeon, *An All-Round Ministry* (Carlisle, Pa.: The Banner of Truth Trust, 1978), 245.

7. Spurgeon, *Lectures to My Students*, vol. 2: 14.

8. Spurgeon, *An All-Round Ministry*, 191.

9. Spurgeon, *Lectures to My Students*, vol. 1: 17.

10. Spurgeon, *Spurgeon's Gems*, 93.

11. Williams, *Personal Reminiscences of Charles Haddon Spurgeon*, 202.

12. Edmond Hez Swem, ed., *Spurgeon's Gold* (New York: Robert Carter & Brothers, 1888), 12.

13. Ibid., 27.

14. Spurgeon, *Lectures to My Students*, vol. 1: 11.

15. Ibid., 11–12.

16. Ibid., 9–10.

17. Ibid., 10.

18. Spurgeon, *An All-Round Ministry*, 247.

19. C. H. Spurgeon, *Counsel for Christian Workers* (Ross-shire, Scotland: Christian Focus Publications, 2001), 116.

20. Swem, ed., *Spurgeon's Gold*, 52.

21. C. H. Spurgeon, *The Greatest Fight in the World*, from The C. H. Spurgeon Collection, version 2.0 (Rio, Wisc.: AGES Software, 2001).

22. Spurgeon, *An All-Round Ministry*, 201–02.

23. Swem, ed., *Spurgeon's Gold*, 53.

24. C. H. Spurgeon, "The Influence of Company," *The Sword and the Trowel (1884)* from The C. H. Spurgeon Collection, version 2.0 (Rio, Wisc.: AGES Software, 2001).

25. Ibid.

26. Spurgeon, *Lectures to My Students*, vol. 1: 14.

27. C. H. Spurgeon, *Flashes of Thought* (London: Passmore & Alabaster, 1888), 204.

28. John Blanchard, ed., *Gathered Gold* (London: Evangelical Press, 1984), 147.

29. John Blanchard, ed., *More Gathered Gold* (London: Evangelical Press, 1984), 151.

30. Spurgeon, *An All-Round Ministry*, 53.

31. Spurgeon, *Flashes of Thought*, 203–04.

32. Ibid., 205.

33. Swem, ed., *Spurgeon's Gold*, 44.

34. Spurgeon, *An All-Round Ministry*, 382.

35. Ibid., 393.

36. Robert Murray McCheyne, as quoted in Spurgeon, *Lectures to My Students*, vol. 1: 2.

37. *C. H. Spurgeon's Prayers* (London: Passmore & Alabaster, 1905), 45–46, 48.

### Chapter 4—A Heart for Service

1. Susannah Spurgeon and J. W. Harrald, *C. H. Spurgeon's Autobiography*, vol. 1 (London: Passmore & Alabaster, 1897), 41.

2. Lewis Drummond, *Spurgeon: Prince of Preachers* (Grand Rapids: Kregel, 1992), 603.

3. Robert Shindler, *From the Pulpit to the Palm Branch* (London: Passmore & Alabaster, 1892), 117–18.

4. C. H. Spurgeon, *The Metropolitan Tabernacle Pulpit*, vol. 3 (London: Passmore & Alabaster, 1857), 241.

5. Spurgeon, *The Metropolitan Tabernacle Pulpit*, vol. 5 (London: Passmore & Alabaster, 1859), 146.

6. Spurgeon, *The Metropolitan Tabernacle Pulpit*, vol. 40 (London: Passmore & Alabaster, 1894), 34.

7. Spurgeon, *The Greatest Fight in the World*, from The C. H. Spurgeon Collection, version 2.0 (Rio, Wisc.: AGES Software, 2001).

8. Lewis Drummond, *Spurgeon: Prince of Preachers*, 288–89.

9. Spurgeon, *The Greatest Fight in the World*.

10. G. Holden Pike, *The Life and Work of Charles Haddon Spurgeon*, vol. 4 (London: Cassell and Company, 1894), 275.

11. "By One Who Knew Him Well," *Charles Haddon Spurgeon: A Biographical Sketch and an Appreciation* (London: Andrew Melrose, 1903), 155.

12. C. H. Spurgeon, *An All-Round Ministry* (Carlisle, Pa.: The Banner of Truth Trust, 1978), 329.

13. *Charles Haddon Spurgeon: A Biographical Sketch*, 156–57.

14. Ibid., 160.

15. Lewis Drummond, *Spurgeon: Prince of Preachers*, 604.

16. C. H. Spurgeon, *Spurgeon's Gems* (London: Passmore & Alabaster, 1859), 166–67.

17. Spurgeon and Harrald, *C. H. Spurgeon's Autobiography*, vol. 1: 144.

18. Ibid., 128; italics in original.

19. Susannah Spurgeon and J. W. Harrald, *C. H. Spurgeon's Autobiography*, vol. 3 (London: Passmore & Alabaster, 1899), 274

20. C. H. Spurgeon, *Lectures to My Students*, vol. 2 (Grand Rapids: Baker, 1987), 22.

21. Spurgeon, *An All-Round Ministry*, 184.

22. *Charles Haddon Spurgeon: A Biographical Sketch*, 160–61.

23. Ibid., 177.

24. Drummond, *Spurgeon: Prince of Preachers*, 432.

25. W. Y. Fullerton, *Charles Haddon Spurgeon* (Chicago, Ill.: Moody, 1966), 135.

26. Ibid., 170.

27. Ibid., 170.

28. C. H. Spurgeon, *Counsel for Christian Workers* (Ross-shire, Scotland: Christian Focus Publications, 2001), 55.

29. Spurgeon, *An All-Round Ministry*, 49.

30. C. H. Spurgeon, *The Check Book of the Bank of Faith* (Fort Washington, Pa.: Christian Literature Crusade, 1960), 48.

31. Spurgeon, *An All-Round Ministry*, 70–71.

32. Spurgeon and Harrald, *C. H. Spurgeon's Autobiography*, vol. 3: 49.

33. Spurgeon, *An All-Round Ministry*, 228–29.

34. Spurgeon and Harrald, *C. H. Spurgeon's Autobiography*, vol. 3: 80–81.

35. James Douglas, *The Prince of Preachers* (London: Morgan and Scott, n.d.), 183.

36. Spurgeon, *The Check Book of the Bank of Faith*, 312.

## Chapter 5—A Love for the Lord and His Word

1.  H. L. Wayland, *Charles H. Spurgeon: His Faith and Works* (Philadelphia: American Baptist Publication Society, 1892), 247.

2.  Charles Ray, *The Life of Charles Haddon Spurgeon* (London: Isbister and Company, 1903), vii.

3.  Iain H. Murray, *Letters of Charles Haddon Spurgeon* (Carlisle, Pa.: The Banner of Truth Trust, 1992), 136.

4.  C. H. Spurgeon, *An All-Round Ministry* (Carlisle, Pa.: The Banner of Truth Trust, 1978), 195.

5.  Susannah Spurgeon and J. W. Harrald, *C. H. Spurgeon's Autobiography*, vol. 1 (London: Passmore & Alabaster, 1897), 4–5.

6.  Ibid., 128.

7.  W. Y. Fullerton, *Charles Haddon Spurgeon* (Chicago, Ill.: Moody, 1966), 171.

8.  J. C. Carlile, *C. H. Spurgeon: An Interpretative Biography* (London: The Religious Tract Society, 1933), 286.

9.  James Douglas, *The Prince of Preachers* (London: Morgan and Scott, n.d.), 102.

10. C. H. Spurgeon, *The New Park Street Pulpit*, vol. 1 (London: Passmore & Alabaster, 1855), 111.

11. Ibid., 110.

12. Edmond Hez Swem, ed., *Spurgeon's Gold* (New York: Robert Carter & Brothers, 1888), 7.

13. Ibid., 53.

14. C. H. Spurgeon, *The Metropolitan Tabernacle Pulpit*, vol. 35 (London: Passmore & Alabaster, 1889), 257.

15. C. H. Spurgeon, *Spurgeon's Gems* (London: Passmore & Alabaster, 1859), 138.

16. Lewis Drummond, *Spurgeon: Prince of Preachers* (Grand Rapids: Kregel, 1992), 570.

17. Spurgeon, *An All-Round Ministry*, 9–10.

18. Ibid., 36.

19. Spurgeon, *The Metropolitan Tabernacle Pulpit*, vol. 26 (London: Passmore & Alabaster, 1880), 50.

20. C. H. Spurgeon, *Counsel for Christian Workers* (Ross-shire, Scotland: Christian Focus Publications, 2001), 95–96.

21. C. H. Spurgeon, *The Greatest Fight in the World*, from The C. H. Spurgeon Collection, version 2.0 (Rio, Wisc.: AGES Software, 2001).

22. Ibid.

23. Ibid.

24. Ibid.

25. Spurgeon, *An All-Round Ministry*, 74–75.

26. *The Pastor in Prayer* (London: Elliot Stock, 1893), 66–67.

**Chapter 6—A Willingness to Suffer**

1. Susannah Spurgeon and J. W. Harrald, *C. H. Spurgeon's Autobiography*, vol. 2 (London: Passmore & Alabaster, 1898), 61.

2. C. H. Spurgeon, *An All-Round Ministry* (Carlisle, Pa.: The Banner of Truth Trust, 1978), 395.

3. C. H. Spurgeon, *Spurgeon's Gems* (London: Passmore & Alabaster, 1859), 8.

4. W. Williams, *Personal Reminiscences of Charles Haddon Spurgeon* (London: The Religious Tract Society, 1895), 200.

5. James Douglas, *The Prince of Preachers* (London: Morgan and Scott, n.d.), 80.

6. Spurgeon and Harrald, *C. H. Spurgeon's Autobiography*, vol. 2: 35.

7. Ibid., 43.

8. Iain H. Murray, *Letters of Charles Haddon Spurgeon* (Carlisle, Pa.: The Banner of Truth Trust, 1992), 194.

9. Lewis Drummond, *Spurgeon: Prince of Preachers* (Grand Rapids: Kregel, 1992), 582.

10. "By One Who Knew Him Well," *Charles Haddon Spurgeon: A Biographical Sketch and an Appreciation* (London: Andrew Melrose, 1903), 166.

11. Susannah Spurgeon and J. W. Harrald, *C. H. Spurgeon's Autobiography*, vol. 3 (London: Passmore & Alabaster, 1899), 197.

12. Spurgeon, *Spurgeon's Gems*, 86.

13. Ibid., 305.

14. Edmond Hez Swem, ed., *Spurgeon's Gold* (New York: Robert Carter & Brothers, 1888), 39.

15. Spurgeon, *Spurgeon's Gems*, 286–87.

16. Ibid., 330.

17. Spurgeon, *Spurgeon's Gems*, 298.

18. Ibid., 299.

19. C. H. Spurgeon, "On My Back," *The Sword and the Trowel* (1867), from The C. H. Spurgeon Collection, version 2.0 (Rio, Wisc.: AGES Software, 2001).

20. C. H. Spurgeon, "Laid Aside. Why?" *The Sword and the Trowel* (1876), from The C. H. Spurgeon Collection.

21. Richard Ellsworth Day, *The Shadow of the Broad Brim* (Philadephia: The Judson Press, 1955), 178.

22. Susannah Spurgeon and J. W. Harrald, *C. H. Spurgeon's Autobiography*, vol. 1 (London: Passmore & Alabaster, 1899), 75.

23. Ibid., 75.

24. Spurgeon, *An All-Round Ministry*, 158.

25. Spurgeon, *Spurgeon's Gems*, 72.

26. Spurgeon, "On My Back," *The Sword and the Trowel* (1867).

27. Spurgeon, "Laid Aside, Why?" The Sword and the Trowel (1867).

28. Ibid.

29. Spurgeon, *An All-Round Ministry*, 384.

30. Spurgeon and Harrald, *C. H. Spurgeon's Autobiography*, vol. 3: 94.

31. Spurgeon, *Spurgeon's Gems*, 36.

32. *The Pastor in Prayer* (London: Eliot Stock, 1893), 74–75.

**Chapter 7—A Zeal for Proclaiming God's Word**

1. Susannah Spurgeon and J. W. Harrald, *C. H. Spurgeon's Autobiography*, vol. 3 (London: Passmore & Alabaster, 1899), 1.

2. Ibid., 356.

3. C. H. Spurgeon, *Lectures to My Students*, vol. 1 (Grand Rapids: Baker, 1987), 82–83.

4. W. Williams, *Personal Reminiscences of Charles Haddon Spurgeon* (London: The Religious Tract Society, 1895), 175.

5. C. H. Spurgeon, *An All-Round Ministry* (Carlisle, Pa.: The Banner of Truth Trust, 1978), 11.

6. Edmond Hez Swem, ed., *Spurgeon's Gold* (New York: Robert Carter & Brothers, 1888), 42.

7. Lecture given by Raymond Brown at William Jewell College, Liberty, Missouri, on the occasion of celebrating the 150th anniversary of Spurgeon's birth (1984), as cited in a Lewis Drummond, *Spurgeon: The Prince of Preachers* (Grand Rapids: Kregel, 1992), 571.

8. Spurgeon, *An All-Round Ministry*, 106–07.

9. C. H. Spurgeon, "What Is It to Win a Soul?" *The Sword and the Trowel, 1879,* from The C. H. Spurgeon Collection, version 2.0 (Rio, Wisc.: AGES Software, 2001).

10. C. H. Spurgeon, *The Sword and the Trowel*, vol. 19 (London: Passmore & Alabaster, 1883), 421.

11. C. H. Spurgeon, *The Greatest Fight in the World*, from The C. H. Spurgeon Collection, version 2.0 (Rio, Wisc.: AGES Software, 2001).

12. Ibid.

13. Lewis Drummond, *Spurgeon: Prince of Preachers* (Grand Rapids: Kregel, 1992), 572.

14. *The Rock*, 5 February 1892, as cited by W. Y. Fullerton, *Charles Haddon Spurgeon* (Chicago, Ill.: Moody, 1966), 224–25.

15. Spurgeon, *Lectures to My Students*, vol. 1: 98–99.

16. "By One Who Knew Him Well," *Charles Haddon Spurgeon: A Biographical Sketch and an Appreciation* (London: Andrew Melrose, 1903), 103.

17. Spurgeon, *Lectures to My Students*, vol. 1: 90.

18. Lecture given by Raymond Brown at William Jewell College, Liberty, Missouri, on the occasion of celebrating the 150th anniversary of Spurgeon's birth.

19. C. H. Spurgeon, "The Christian Minister's Private Prayer," *The Sword and the Trowel* (1868), from The C. H. Spurgeon Collection.

20. Spurgeon, *An All-Round Ministry*, 329.

21. Susannah Spurgeon and J. W. Harrald, *C. H. Spurgeon's Autobiography*, vol. 2 (London: Passmore & Alabaster, 1899), 335.

22. Williams, *Personal Reminiscences of Charles Haddon Spurgeon*, 174.

23. C. H. Spurgeon, *Spurgeon's Gems* (London: Passmore & Alabaster, 1859), 280.

24. Spurgeon, *Lectures to My Students*, vol. 1: 98.

25. Williams, *Personal Reminiscences of Charles Haddon Spurgeon*, 173.

26. Spurgeon, *An All-Round Ministry*, 74.

27. Ibid., 348.

28. Williams, *Personal Reminiscences of Charles Haddon Spurgeon*, 174.

29. Spurgeon, *An All-Round Ministry*, 111–12.

30. Spurgeon, *Lectures to My Students*, vol. 1: 72.

31. Williams, *Personal Reminiscences of Charles Haddon Spurgeon*, 134.

32. Drummond, *Spurgeon: Prince of Preachers*, 452.

33. W. Y. Fullerton, *Charles Haddon Spurgeon* (Chicago, Moody, 1966), 189.

34. Williams, *Personal Reminiscences of Charles Haddon Spurgeon*, 145.

35. Spurgeon, *Spurgeon's Gems*, 73.

36. J. B. Weatherspoon, "Charles Haddon Spurgeon," *The Review and Expositor*, vol. 31: 411.

37. Drummond, *Spurgeon: Prince of Preachers*, 295.

38. Spurgeon, *Spurgeon's Gems*, 202.

39. Spurgeon, *Lectures to My Students*, vol 1:85.

40. James Douglas, *The Prince of Preachers* (London: Morgan and Scott, n.d.), 131–32.

41. Williams, *Personal Reminiscences of Charles Haddon Spurgeon*, 191.

42. C. H. Spurgeon, *Lectures to My Students*, vol. 2: 3.

43. Ibid., 4–5.

44. Ibid., 4.

45. Spurgeon, *The Greatest Fight in the World*, from The C. H. Spurgeon Collection.

46. Spurgeon, *An All-Round Ministry*, 339–40.

47. C. H. Spurgeon, *Lectures to My Students*, vol. 2: 11.

48. Ibid., 12.

49. Ibid., 12.

50. C. H. Spurgeon, *Lectures to My Students*, vol. 1: 88.

51. Ibid.

52. C. H. Spurgeon, "Your Best Always," *The Sword and the Trowel* (1883), from The C. H. Spurgeon Collection.

53. Spurgeon, *An All-Round Ministry*, 362.

54. Spurgeon, *Lectures to My Students*, vol. 1: 72–74.

**Chapter 8—A Passion for Lost Souls**

1. Susannah Spurgeon and J. W. Harrald, *C. H. Spurgeon's Autobiography*, vol. 1 (London: Passmore & Alabaster, 1897), 124.

2. Robert Shindler, *From the Usher's Desk to the Tabernacle Pulpit* (London: Passmore & Alabaster, 1892), 186.

3. C. H. Spurgeon, *Around the Wicket Gate* (London: Passmore & Alabaster, 1890), 16.

4. Robert Shindler, *From the Pulpit to the Palm Branch* (London: Passmore & Alabaster, 1892), 121.

5. W. Y. Fullerton, *Charles Haddon Spurgeon* (Chicago: Moody, 1966), 227–28.

6. Ibid., 191.

7. C. H. Spurgeon, "What Is It to Win a Soul?" *The Sword and the Trowel* (1879), from The C. H. Spurgeon Collection, version 2.0 (Rio, Wisc.: AGES Software, 2001).

8. C. H. Spurgeon, *An All-Round Ministry* (Carlisle, Pa.: The Banner of Truth Trust, 1978), 248.

9. Edmond Hez Swem, ed., *Spurgeon's Gold* (New York: Robert Carter & Brothers, 1888), 33.

10. Iain H. Murray, *Letters of Charles Haddon Spurgeon* (Carlisle, Pa.: The Banner of Truth Trust, 1992), 136.

11. John Blanchard, *More Gathered Gold* (London: Evangelical Press, 1986), 308.

12. Spurgeon, *An All-Round Ministry*, 192.

13. Ibid., 194.

14. Swem, ed., *Spurgeon's Gold*, 32.

15. Spurgeon, *An All-Round Ministry*, 236–37.

16. John Blanchard, *Gathered Gold* (London: Evangelical Press, 1984), 299.

17. C. H. Spurgeon, *Counsel for Christian Workers* (Ross-shire, Scotland: Christian Focus Publications, 2001), 114–15.

18. C. H. Spurgeon, *The Metropolitan Tabernacle Pulpit*, vol. 44 (London: Passmore & Alabaster, 1898), 296.

19. Spurgeon, *An All-Round Ministry*, 63–64.

20. W. Williams, *Personal Reminiscences of Charles Haddon Spurgeon* (London: The Religious Tract Society, 1895), 178.

21. Spurgeon, *An All-Round Ministry*, 365.

22. C. H. Spurgeon, *Spurgeon's Gems* (London: Passmore & Alabaster, 1859), 201–02.

23. C. H. Spurgeon, *Counsel for Christian Workers*, 17–18.

24. Ibid., 9.

25. Spurgeon, *An All-Round Ministry*, 70.

26. Ibid., 343.

27. Fullerton, *Charles Haddon Spurgeon*, 276.

28. William Cowper, *There Is a Fountain Filled with Blood*, verses 3–4. The lines of verse 4 are reversed in some hymnal editions; this is the order shown on Spurgeon's tombstone.

29. Spurgeon and Harrald, *C. H. Spurgeon's Autobiography*, vol. 1:180.

30. Ibid., 135.

### Conclusion—The Power of a Single Focus

1. C. H. Spurgeon, *The Check Book of the Bank of Faith* (Fort Washington, Pa.: Christian Literature Crusade, 1960), 48.

2. C. H. Spurgeon, *The Metropolitan Tabernacle Pulpit*, vol. 10 (London: Passmore & Alabaster, 1864), 87.

3. C. H. Spurgeon, *Lectures to My Students*, vol. 2 (Grand Rapids: Baker, 1987), 22.

4. C. H. Spurgeon, *Counsel for Christian Workers* (Ross-shire, Scotland: Christian Focus Publications, 2001), 70.

5. C. H. Spurgeon, *Spurgeon's Gems* (London: Passmore & Alabaster, 1859), 14–15.

6. C. H. Spurgeon, *An All-Round Ministry* (Carlisle, Pa.: The Banner of Truth Trust, 1978), 33.

7. Ibid., 49.

8. Ibid., 274–75.

9. Susannah Spurgeon and J. W. Harrald, *C. H. Spurgeon's Autobiography*, vol. 1 (London: Passmore & Alabaster, 1897), 180.

# Further Reading on C. H. Spurgeon

∞

If after reading this book you find you would like to read Spurgeon's lectures and sermons to pastors and his Pastors' College students, an excellent place to start is his book *An All-Round Ministry*, reprinted the The Banner of Truth Trust. You can also read *Lectures to My Students*, which was originally published in three separate volumes but recently brought together into one volume by Baker Book House.

As for biographies, my personal favorite is *Charles Haddon Spurgeon* by W. Y. Fullerton and reprinted by Moody Publishers. Fullerton knew Spurgeon personally and did an excellent job of providing a concise overview of the key areas of Spurgeon's life. A more lengthy and in-depth biography is Lewis Drummond's *Spurgeon: Prince of Preachers*, published by Kregel Publications.

## *C. H. Spurgeon on Spiritual Leadership Team*

**Acquiring Editor:**
Mark Tobey

**Copy Editor:**
Jim Vincent

**Back Cover Copy:**
Julie-Allyson Ieron, Joy Media

**Cover Design:**
Smartt Guys Design

**Interior Design:**
Paetzold Associates

**Printing and Binding:**
Versa Press Inc.

*The typeface for the text of this book is*
***Berkeley***